Last of the Saddle Tramps

One woman's seven thousand mile
equestrian odyssey

by

Messanie Wilkins

The Long Riders' Guild Press

www.thelongridersguild.com

ISBN: 1-59048-043-0

To the Reader:

The editors and publishers of The Long Riders' Guild Press faced significant technical and financial difficulties in bringing this and the other titles in the Equestrian Travel Classics collection to the light of day.

Though the authors represented in this international series envisioned their stories being shared for generations to come, all too often that was not the case. Sadly, many of the books now being published by The Long Riders' Guild Press were discovered gracing the bookshelves of rare book dealers, adorned with princely prices that placed them out of financial reach of the common reader. The remainder were found lying neglected on the scrap heap of history, their once-proud stories forgotten, their once-glorious covers stained by the toil of time and a host of indifferent previous owners.

However The Long Riders' Guild Press passionately believes that this book, and its literary sisters, remain of global interest and importance. We stand committed, therefore, to bringing our readers the best copy of these classics at the most affordable price. The copy which you now hold may have small blemishes originating from the master text.

We apologize in advance for any defects of this nature.

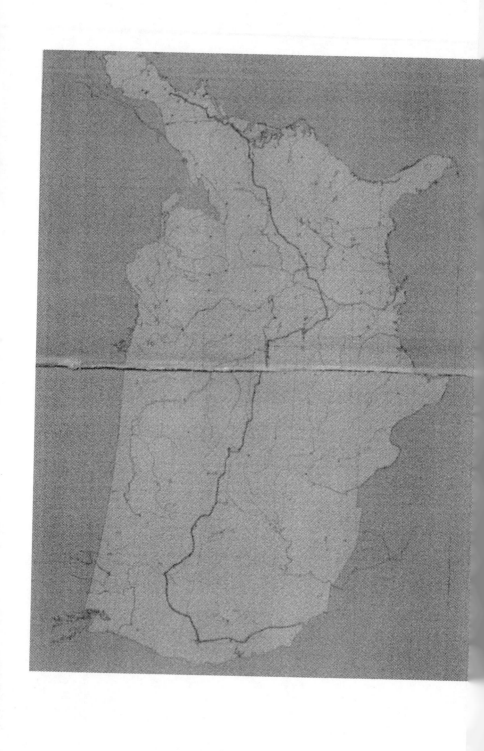

CONTENTS

1 ☞ MINOT, MAINE

I was born in Minot, Maine and lived there for the most part until I was five weeks shy of my sixty-third year, by which time it seemed pointless to remain. The decision to leave all I'd ever known and loved was the hardest one I'd ever made, but the Lord helped me make it, so I knew I was doing the right thing. Still, even with His help, it took me quite a spell to make up my mind. Maine women don't rush into things.

"California, here we come," I said on that morning in November. The only ones who heard me were my dog and my horse. They didn't understand, of course, but from the way they looked at me I could tell they sensed something more than winter was in the wind. Had they known the meaning of my words, I suppose both of them would have hightailed it over the nearest hill. We loved each other, but they were far too smart to walk all the way to California just to satisfy an old woman's foolish whim.

I admit that I felt sort of foolish. I was dressed for comfort in the saddle and safety on the road, and that added up to male attire: A hunting cap with ear flaps, a blanket-lined vest over a wool shirt, heavy work jeans, and rubbers over lumberman's felt boots. This was the visible Mesannie. Next to my skin was a wool union suit.

My horse's name was Tarzan, but on that morning he looked like an open moving van. He was piled high with everything essential to our journey, or just about everything that I still owned. The only clear space on his back was twelve inches of saddle where I intended to rest my sixty-one inches and one hundred and fifty pounds. My pockets were stuffed with gear, so my true weight was closer to two hundred.

I don't know how old Tarzan was. He was aged, but he wasn't a complainer. Depeche Toi, my dog, was fourteen months. With a name like that, you might think he was a Poodle, but he wasn't. The shaggy little brown and white was mostly Spaniel and Dachshund, or so I'd been told.

"All I ask of you is patience," I said to my two companions. "We're heading off for a long walk, but someday we'll settle down. I promise."

The someday I had in mind was twenty-five months away, when I'd be sixty-five and eligible for old age benefits. I didn't tell them that, nor did I tell them that when and if we settled down, why it wouldn't be for long.

Months back, my doctor at the hospital had told me that I had two to four years to live, "If you live restfully."

I figured I'd get plenty of rest in the saddle. I couldn't rest in my house because the bank was taking over.

I'd lived most of my life in that little house. First with my parents, then with my mother and Uncle Waldo, and finally alone.

"We won't get to California standing around here." I put my left foot in the stirrup, swung my right leg up and over, and settled down on the saddle. Tarzan swung around and walked toward the road. The dog trotted along behind us. I put my hand in one pocket to make sure that our bankroll of thirty-two dollars was there. It was.

The road that ran past my ancestral farm was called an endroad in Maine. A plain dirt road running off a paved road, and the farm sat back almost a mile from the traffic. Minot had one snowplow for its hundred and eight miles of roads, and my endroad was always the last one to be plowed.

Now, as we walked down that endroad for the last time, I didn't have the heart to look back at my little house. (I don't imagine I will ever see it again.)

We hadn't progressed a hundred yards when I started having the jitters. I'd been convincing myself for weeks that my plan was a wise one, but now, only a hundred yards from home, I wasn't so sure. What sort of an idiot am I anyway? Thirty-two dollars wouldn't get us to California, and who in his right mind would hire an old woman to work at odd jobs along the way? If the newspapers were right, plenty of men were out of work, so who would hire a complete stranger, an old woman who dressed like a man?

I came close to calling the whole thing off right then and there. Nobody was forcing me to leave Maine. My own home was gone, but there were people who would help me, and one in particular—an old school friend of my mother's, who'd offered me her home.

"Best way to overcome the shakes is to talk your fool head off," had been Uncle Waldo's advice, which may have been why he was so talkative. So I started talking:

"My ancestors were pioneers and that's something to remember if we get into trouble, because Stuarts and Libbys and Shillings are spread out in every state. See that old stone fence there? Slave labor. White slaves. Poor people who came over here from Europe, so they had to work off the passage money. Some never did earn their freedom. The slaves around here belonged to Mickel Little, who was deeded all the land by King's Grant. One of the slaves became a freedman by marrying Mickel's daughter. That Mickel was a wild one—fought both Indians and whites—and Maine would just as soon forget him. Edward Little is the one we remember. There's a school in Auburn named after him, with a statue of him out front. See that gully over to the left? I can remember when they used to call it 'The Slut's Hole' in honor of an old she-wolf who had a den down there. Never saw her myself. Wolves used to be common here in Maine. But don't you two worry. Wolves have changed." That wasn't all I said. Just a sampler.

Uncle Waldo's prescription worked fine. My confidence had flowed back by the time we reached the hard road and turned toward Hackett's Mill. Minot was at our backs, and I felt we were leaving it forever. I'd been thinking about this very moment for days, wondering if I might cry when I reached it.

I didn't. It should have been a moment of great sentiment, but I felt no touch of sadness. Instead, I felt a great surge of release, as if I had been one of Mickel Little's slaves who had just won her freedom. It wasn't a feeling against Minot. All in all, I'd had a fine life there, only the recent years had been real troublesome, and no one was to blame for them.

The only hope I had on my mind was that the minister wouldn't come along in his car. If he did, he'd surely stop and ask questions, and it would take me an hour to explain. What would be his reaction when I told him the way the Lord had helped me make my decision?

But the minister didn't come along, so he and I were both spared.

No one could have convinced me that I was doing the wrong thing. I'd lived through enough Maine winters, and I didn't think I could survive another one, especially the one coming up. The wild geese had been honking their way south earlier than usual, and I hadn't heard or seen a crow in six weeks.

I was so tired of being alone. I wanted to be among people, but I knew they would have to be strangers so that when I found work, they wouldn't think they owned me body and soul for the rest of my life.

In a way, I was three decades late in starting for California. I can still hear my mother saying, "I wish that sometime we could hitch up the horse, pack in what we could carry, and just we three go like the gypsies—only work, not steal, along

4

the way." She started saying that when it looked as if we couldn't hold the farm, and the "three" she referred to were herself, myself and Uncle Waldo. My father had died years before during prohibition. Her words "along the way" meant along the way to California.

Mama had never been there, but a friend of hers had and told her all about it. If I had encouraged her, perhaps we would have made the journey. Chances would have been slim, though. Uncle Waldo was older than my mother and she respected his opinions, and nothing would have budged him from Maine. He didn't recognize any other state.

His opinions about farming were rigid, too. Mama and I followed his advice, and within two years we were both working a fifty-six-hour week in the shoe shop at Auburn. Each of us earned three dollars and sixty-five cents a week. Uncle Waldo looked out for things on the farm. He was a hard worker, but not the speediest farmer in Maine. We lent assistance Saturday afternoon and Sundays, plus evenings when necessary. Picking sweet corn for the canning factory and hauling hay were always done by moonlight or the tasks wouldn't have been completed.

We were doing well and planning to buy some farm equipment when a truck ran into me and injured the horse I was driving. The horse had to be put down, and I landed in the hospital with a fracture between the knee and ankle of one leg. First the doctors thought they wouldn't be able to save my leg, but they did. It meant a seven months' stay in the hospital.

Laws were different in those days and not all drivers were insured. I was unable to collect damages. So it was an expensive hospital stay, and while I was there a greater tragedy occurred. My mother died.

After that, it was downhill most of the way. My leg healed slowly and wasn't much good for two years. We lost everything except the farm itself, and without livestock, farming was out of the question. Uncle Waldo was going on seventy-seven when he found work on a W.P.A. project. He earned

5

a reputation as one of the best workers, and went eighteen months without missing a day. I heard a lot about what the W.P.A. did in some other places, but they certainly worked on that project. No loafing with Uncle Waldo's boss, who was the road commissioner and he intended to hold that title for the next year.

One thing we learned from that job was how to make a little meat go a long way. Uncle Waldo was a proud man, and it embarrassed him when he discovered that all the other workers brought meat sandwiches for lunch. So he'd walk down the road and eat his lunch alone, because he didn't have meat in his sandwiches. We were saving money to buy chickens at the time, and home meals were mostly beans and cornmeal. Well, I solved his social difficulty by buying some ground meat and making a loaf out of one-third meat and two-thirds cereal. Then I sliced the loaf and put it in his sandwiches. They looked all meat, and after that he lunched with the other men.

They made Uncle Waldo retire when he was seventy-eight. He thought they were wrong and proved it by finding odd jobs around Minot. The jobs never paid more than a dollar for a ten-hour day, and often that meant a three- or four-mile walk for him, but he didn't turn anything down.

The money he earned went into our farm, and we started to see some profit in the future. Come spring, we'd have some saleable heifers and gilts and old hens, and the income would cover the feed bills and leave something to spare for personal needs. The farm would be a going proposition.

But winter changed things around. Uncle Waldo was going blind from cataracts. He went into the hospital, but they sent him home, saying he was too old and weak to stand an operation. His vision was fading fast, and I had all the work to do. Still, that didn't change the promise of spring.

What did was the grippe, or flu, as some called it. There was an epidemic around, and it hit me. I'd had grippe before, but this time it grew into pneumonia, and the doctor ordered

6

me to stay in bed. It was sound advice, but somebody had to care for the livestock. I was that somebody.

Well, I could hardly get to the barn. I kept falling down in the snow from being so dizzy. Uncle Waldo helped some, and we managed to get enough wood into the house to keep warm. He couldn't see well enough to split it, and I didn't have the strength. Except for the visits to the barn, I followed the doctor's orders.

Then we went through a blizzard. It drifted all the roads, and Minot's only snowplow had a time of it plowing according to the law: Main roads and mail routes first, except in cases of emergency.

Uncle Waldo and I were isolated for a week. The congestion in my lungs worsened and I was in great pain. I needed my doctor, but there was nothing either of us could do to get word to him. Even if we'd had a horse, Uncle Waldo wouldn't have been able to get through the drifts on our unplowed endroad. All I could do was pray that somebody would come along. All Uncle Waldo could do was talk, and he did that night and day, so I knew he was just as frightened as I was.

When I heard voices one evening, I was in no condition to recognize them. My nearest neighbor, a French farmer down our road a piece, had snowshoed over with his two boys to see how things were going with us. I wouldn't be writing this now if that man hadn't snowshoed to the main road and phoned for both the plow and my doctor.

The plow came first, then the doctor, then an ambulance. They took me to the hospital, and I was there three weeks. From there I went to a nursing home, with orders to stay put until spring. X-rays showed spots on one lung which the doctor couldn't explain.

The French boys had stayed on with Uncle Waldo for a few days, caring for him and the livestock, but then other arrangements had to be made for Uncle Waldo. He went to a nursing home for old people and there was no one left on the farm. The farm stock was sold for whatever it would

7

bring. When you have to sell in a hurry, you don't get much.

The boys took Depeche Toi, which means Hurry Up, home with them. They'd given him to me the previous year, when he was just a little pup. They gave him his name, too. A good name. The dog was always in a hurry, especially when he needed out and was waiting at the door.

Uncle Waldo never did return to the farm. He died in the nursing home.

But I returned in mid-spring, thanks to a little lying. I told people that I felt better than I really did, and fooled enough of them, although I can't say I pulled the wool over my doctor's eyes. "All right, Mesannie," he told me, "I'll permit you to go home on one condition: Rest. Be as inactive as possible. That lung of yours worries me, and it should worry you. I want you to remind yourself of these two words every day: Live Restfully. Now I don't mean to frighten you, but you have two to four more years ahead of you—if you live restfully. So will you promise to take it easy?"

"I'm not one to pay for information and then disregard it," I assured him, avoiding the word "promise". I never did believe in lying to a doctor, and the word "disregard" has all sorts of latitude.

Two days later, the doctor drove me home. When he left he reminded me to check with him every two weeks, and to live restfully for the rest of my life. So there I was, home again and broke again—no stock and no money—and the only hope in sight was a contract with a pickle company to raise cucumbers. They furnished the seed and fertilizer, and the cost was applied against the total they paid for the cucumbers in the fall. My whole future was in pickles, and somehow I had to get through to the fall.

I was alone on the farm except for Depeche Toi, and I didn't know just how I could get through. It was the lowest period of my life, a time when I felt weak and depressed and nervous. I left a door open at night so the dog wouldn't be trapped inside in case I died.

One day I noticed sweet ferns in the pasture. With strips of

8

paper from a bag, I made cigarettes from the ferns and smoked three, one after the other. I'd read some place that sweet fern cigarettes were good for the nerves. They helped me, no doubt about that. I was sixty-two and smoking for the first time.

The biggest help came unexpectedly and from friends. In late May, a friend from Upper Gloucester came over to harrow the ground and plant my cucumber seeds. A neighbor cultivated the plants for me the first time, but after that I was on my own to weed, hoe, dust and pick. I had a big piece planted, for I'd expected to work the field with help, so I had to keep going, rain or shine. There was no time to fix a hot meal. The dog and I would take lunch and a pail of water to the field.

A neighbor farmer cut my hay on shares that year, and the French boys came over to help me get mine in. I don't know why I kept any of it. Just habit, I guess. I didn't have any stock to eat the hay.

I was feeling stronger at cucumber-picking time. I was told that one person couldn't possibly pick them alone, but I knew that if I hired help I wouldn't have enough money to winter on. So I picked every day, rain or shine, from dawn until darkness. I had to, because nothing in the world grows as fast as a cucumber, and those under four inches bring the best price.

Every night, I'd grade the cucumbers by lantern. Then I'd have a late supper and fall into bed, completely exhausted. And all the time, I tried not to think about the doctor's advice about getting plenty of rest. It wasn't difficult. I was too tired to think.

Luck was on my side for a change. The frosts didn't hit my land until October, and the truck kept coming back to pick up my cucumbers. It was a short-crop year elsewhere, so the prices paid were high. I ended up with a few more dollars than I'd anticipated. Enough to winter on.

This should have been a comforting thought, but it wasn't. When you're alone, home isn't home anymore. The winter to come would be the first to find me alone in my little house. Remembering the blizzard, I knew I didn't want to risk being isolated again. If my house on the endroad would be safe for an old woman, then it would have to be for some other old woman. I didn't intend to die there all alone.

That's when I started thinking about wandering south, and about my mother's old wish of going to California by horse and buggy. Times and prices had changed, and I knew a buggy would be too expensive for me. But a horse? I hadn't ridden a horse in over thirty years. Still, if I was going to travel to a warmer clime, my own two feet wouldn't get me very far.

I had plenty of time to think, but I needed only a few minutes to develop a simple, rational plan. I would buy the cheapest horse I could find, ride him south until my money gave out, find a job, save a few dollars, and then ride on. The goal would be my mother's goal: California.

All I needed was encouragement.

I explained the whole plan to Depeche Toi, but if he reacted one way or another, I didn't notice. I was just practicing on him anyway, figuring out just what to say when I discussed my plan with two of my mother's old school friends. I could trust them not to gossip. I didn't want everybody in Minot to know my business.

Mrs. Williams thought I was joking. She was in her nineties and had never been married, so I don't know why she was called Mrs. Williams, but everybody had done just that for as long as I could remember.

"I'm not joking," I told her.

"Yes you are," she insisted. "And let me remind you, Mesannie Mabel Libby Wilkins, you don't have the courage your mother had, for she was a true Libby of the old strain, and even she didn't have the gumption to go to California. And how long has it been since you've been on a horse? And furthermore, there's not a safe road in America anymore!"

10

"I was thinking of using secondary roads. I'm in no hurry."

"Why, you couldn't begin to carry the things you'd need on a horse! You'd need a buggy, and the wheels wouldn't last very long. No, you must be joking. You've been a lady all your life, Mesannie Mabel! Don't ruin your reputation at this late stage. And don't mention this to anyone else, or you'll find yourself being sent up to Augusta."

Augusta, of course, was where the state had its insane asylum. I promised Mrs. Williams that I wouldn't tell anyone else, and then called on my mother's other old friend, Mrs. Miller. Mrs. Williams and Mrs. Miller hadn't spoken to each other in forty years. Why, I don't know. People said that even those two had forgotten why.

Mrs. Miller poured tea and kept nodding her head as she heard me out. "This doesn't surprise me one bit," she said. "While you were talking, I was thinking of your Grandma Libby."

Grandma Libby had been almost eighty when she rode from South Auburn to Bangor and back again, stopping only to change horses and swimming the river twice. A hundred and eighty miles in just under thirty hours. She surprised many men, and several horses, I imagine.

"So this sort of thing is in your bloodstream," continued Mrs. Miller, "and if I were your age and a Libby, I'd have a notion to join you. Didn't your family have a Shilling on the Lewis and Clark expedition? If you get out there, you should try to ride some of that trail. So I think you're doing something wonderful, Mesannie. You can do it, so long as you think you can do it. You may be tired and hungry lots of times, but trust in God, keep going, and you'll get there. And don't feel too bad about leaving Minot. All you've had here was hard work and misfortune. So go right ahead, and I hope you'll come back to see me sometime. Too bad I don't have horses anymore, but I'm not clairvoyant. Now if things go wrong, or if they go right and you want to come back, remember that this is a big house and there'll always be plenty of room for you."

11

She didn't offer me any money, and I didn't ask for any. Her encouragement was just what I needed and worth more than money.

So I started looking around for a horse. It was the right time of year to find a bargain, for summer camps and rental stables would be trying to reduce non-seasonal overhead. By letter, I answered a riding academy's advertisement in the local paper and explained what I wanted in a horse: A tough one, sex and disposition unimportant, with looks I wouldn't be ashamed of, and wearing the lowest possible price tag.

The academy was near Portland, some forty miles away. The owners answered my letter by calling on me, then they drove me to their place to see a horse they thought would fill my requirements. They were so anxious to sell the horse that I figured he would be a lemon, but I was wrong.

Tarzan was a rusty black of fourteen-plus hands and he looked pretty good to me. Eyes wide apart, ears small and pointed, nicely shaped feet and strong, clean legs. He was well built, and reminded me of the old-time trotters that used to race at our fairs. I knew that his scrawny neck was due to light feed and overwork.

The horse stood like a statue while I mounted him, and he had a nice, easy walk. I felt right at home on him and said so.

"When you feel like that on a horse," said one of the sellers, "then he is the horse for you. You could ride ten thousand and not find a better one."

In all truth, I couldn't have found a better horse for my purpose if I'd paid ten thousand dollars. A stupid horse would be hard on me, and a mean one might kill me with the rig I had. Tarzan was extremely intelligent. I knew I had to have him, and I think I would have paid my last dollar for him. The price nearly came to that, too.

They trucked him over to my place and we spent the next few days getting acquainted. Right off, he and Depeche Toi took to each other. It was love at first sight between those two.

I was considerably younger than the artillery saddle. It had seen better days, and I hoped that it would hold where it was mended. I stripped it down to make it as light as possible: A single strap to the stirrups, no hood and no skirts. The collar was an ancient one, too. I rived it good so there'd be no rough rivet heads to chafe my horse. His bits were straight ones, so that he could eat at any time.

It didn't take too long to get Tarzan's tack in shape, and then I started planning just what to take along. I made a list and kept scratching things off and then adding them on again. I was still planning when the calendar changed to November, and I could feel winter in my bones. Otherwise, I felt fine.

The days from the last of the cucumbers to November had been restful, more or less, as the doctor had ordered. There was no sound reason to delay our start, except that I was debating whether or not to talk things over with my minister. I don't know what I expected from him, but I'd been a religious woman all of my life, and I suppose I held back for fear he'd try to talk me out of my journey. He was a practical man.

I walked to town one day and bought a diary. I was sure that I'd meet the minister on the street, and then I'd tell him my plans. When I didn't run into him, my problem was solved. Fate had kept me from informing him.

The diary was so that I would have something to do on the long journey to the far coast. Writing in it and reading from it would give me something to do on lonely nights. It was my one luxury item. The cost was sixty cents.

It was the sixth of November. I was ready to go and planned on an early morning start, rain or shine. I went to bed extra early that night, determined to get a restful, long sleep.

But all sorts of memories and anxieties crowded my mind after I'd said my usual prayer. So I prayed again and found myself asking, "Does what I'm doing meet with Your approval? Am I doing the right thing?" I didn't expect an answer, but I sort of expected some sign. If one came, I didn't recognize it, so I said, "I know You are busy, but if I toss a coin five times and it comes up heads three-out-of-five, will that mean I have Your approval?"

I didn't wait for a sign. I climbed out of bed, turned on a light, found a coin and then flipped it. It came up heads four times out of five! So I had His approval!

I put out the light and went back to bed. "Thank You," I said. I had no trouble at all falling asleep.

The early start had turned into a late one, because I'd had trouble stowing all the gear on Tarzan. I had a lot to learn about tying things so they wouldn't slip. I was using string where rope or regular tie straps would have been better, but I didn't own straps or rope.

So we had unexpected stops along the hard road to Hackett's Mill. Tarzan took his work seriously, and every time he felt something slipping off his flanks, he'd halt and turn his head and look at me. I'd fix things and we'd take off again. Depeche Toi stayed reasonably close. He was used to traffic, having been at the nursing home with me, so I wasn't worried about him.

At Hackett's Mill, we made a few planned stops so that I could say goodbye to old friends. Now that I was on my way, I didn't care how fast the gossip traveled or what anyone said about me. Just as I'd anticipated, my friends told me I was attempting a foolish thing. I'm sure a couple of them would have called it sinful, but they didn't want to offend me.

From there, we turned off toward Minot Corner, where I'd stayed in the nursing home. It was a side trip of six miles, but I wanted to say goodbye to a few of the people there, too. It meant crossing a wooden bridge, and I knew that wouldn't bother Tarzan, but when we came to it I found a new cement bridge. Nobody along the way had mentioned the new bridge to me. I suppose they thought the whole world knew about it.

Tarzan took the bridge in stride, but an hour later (on the return trip) he had a change of mind. He stopped and

14

snorted, laid his ears back and whirled around a few times. Depeche Toi moved in close, as if to keep Tarzan from bolting, but the horse kept dancing in circles and turning fast on his hind feet. It takes a good rider to stay aboard when a horse does that. I was a rusty, poor rider. I hung onto Tarzan's mane for dear life. When the dog started barking, I could have crowned him. Then I was all for kissing him, for the barks had a soothing effect on the horse. Tarzan quieted right down, and just in time. A few more turns and he'd have lost me and all the gear.

A couple of men had started crossing the bridge on foot, so we'd had an audience all that time. I felt a little ashamed to ask one of them to lead Tarzan across the bridge, but I did. The man obliged, and Tarzan went along as calm as you please. After that, he was never skittish about cement bridges.

From there we went down a road that was new to me. It ran south and wasn't on a direct line for California, but it would lead us to the home of my friend in Upper Gloucester. That was my goal for the first day in the saddle.

It was well past noon when we passed a yard where a lady was cutting flowers. I knew my helpers were hungry, but all I wanted was a cup of tea, and a chance to stretch my legs. We stopped and I asked the lady for some hot water. Never saw her before in my life, but she insisted that I have lunch with her. First I fed Tarzan and Depeche Toi, and then the lady and I had a fine lunch and a pleasant visit.

"You'll like California," she told me. "Lovely people."

"You've been there?"

"No, but last summer a man and his wife had a flat tire right in front of my house. They were from California. Lovely people. I wish I were going with you."

After our stop, Tarzan was anxious to step up the pace. I had a time holding him in. He seemed to know that Upper Gloucester was quite a way yet and he was in a hurry to get there. I didn't blame him, with the load he was carrying—including me.

Depeche Toi stayed well up ahead of us. He made it his

business to scout every yard on both sides of the road. Then he visited one yard where he wasn't welcome. He came running back to me, yipping all the way, with a big, unfriendly dog at his heels.

My dog ran right under Tarzan's belly. The horse snorted, laid his ears back, and went up on his hind feet. When he came down, his front hoofs seemed to be reaching for Depeche Toi's pursuer. The big dog yelped, tucked his tail between his legs, and ran for home. When we passed his house, he was nowhere in sight. I was pleased to know that my horse would defend my dog, and hoped he would do the same for me, if need be.

It was near dark when we reached Upper Gloucester. I asked several people how to get to my friend's house. They all knew where it was, but no two agreed on just how to get there. So it was after dark when we found the place, and a warm welcome awaited us.

Tarzan had done all the work, yet he seemed the freshest. The dog had covered about ten times as much ground, and he was all tuckered out. I was somewhere in between.

The night before, I'd made the first entry in my diary: "I start tomorrow, on Friday, leaving home and friends behind. I go forth as a tramp of fate among strangers."

On this night I wrote: "Covered twenty-one miles today, but not all in the right direction. We're three miles closer to California."

2 🐎 MAINE

We started out early in the morning and carried more than the day before. My friend gave us a supply of food, a stack of hay, grain, and some money. The gifts were important, for now we could put more distance between us and the coming winter before I had to start job hunting.

I walked Tarzan through the village. He matched his pace to mine and kept his nose to me, as if he'd been doing it all his life. The hay over his flanks was bulky and made him look high in the rear.

I kept Depeche Toi on a leash that was made of old cotton clothesline. The way he'd run the day before, I was afraid his legs would wear out in no time. Still, he was full of life, and I envied him. I was stiff all over, so I walked for awhile, trying to get my legs in working order.

Once clear of the village, I got back into the saddle and we headed down the main highway that runs from Lewiston to Portland. I tied the dog's lead rope to the saddle, and he trailed along behind us for awhile, just as if he'd been trained to do so. I wanted to break him of the habit of running into every dooryard that we passed.

17

The system worked well for ten minutes or so. Then Depeche Toi decided that if he couldn't visit yards he'd at least investigate every telephone pole. I didn't mind until he wound himself around two poles in a row and we had to wait until he unwound himself. I shortened the rope so he couldn't reach any poles, or we wouldn't have made more than two miles that day. I wanted to keep him in close anyway, because traffic had picked up and cars were whizzing by.

I was keeping my eyes on the cars and trucks, so when Tarzan came to a sudden halt I didn't know why. Depeche Toi had circled the horse twice and had him more or less hogtied. So I sat there, determined not to dismount, and tried to coax the dog into reversing his circles and freeing Tarzan's legs. It didn't work, but a car pulled to the side of the highway and the driver came over and unwound Depeche Toi. When I thanked him, he asked how far I was going.

"Quite a piece," I told him.

"If it's not too inconvenient, I'd suggest using some other road. It's dangerous for you, and traffic will be heavier later on."

"I plan on cutting off to the west at Gray."

"Fine. That's less than three miles. Good luck."

I shortened the dog's rope to about twelve feet, and we started on our way again. This time, Depeche Toi trotted out in front of us and stayed there. People laughed and waved as they drove by us. I suppose we did look like a small parade: The little dog leading the big horse with the lady tramp on top.

We turned off at Gray, but the traffic didn't lessen. The road was being used as a detour, but nobody had told me that. Still, drivers were polite and gave us plenty of room. Then we hit a wooded strip where the road narrowed and there was hardly any shoulder. Up ahead and coming for us, one car was passing another, and a truck with canvas flying was trying to pass them both. As the truck cut right in front of us, Depeche Toi jumped the road shoulder. The canvas flapped right in Tarzan's face. He reared and headed for the

18

trees. Then he stopped and lowered his head to nibble some weeds. Tarzan was reacting as if nothing had happened, but I was still shaking, and wondered how the gear and I had stayed on!

There'd been a witness: An old farmer mending a fence line. Now he walked over to us and said, "There's terror on the roads these days." When I nodded, he added, "I can see you know horses, and from your outfit I'd say you might be looking for work. It so happens I could use some help for a couple of weeks. Interested?"

I wanted to laugh. I'd spent hours worrying about my chances of finding a job among strangers, and here—on my second day—a stranger was offering me a job. Now, before answering him, I took off my cap. I'd cut my white hair short, but he was no longer fooled.

"Why, you're a woman!" he said. "Thought you were a man."

"Does that mean that your need for help has flown the coop?"

"Not at all," he chuckled. "You can handle a horse better than most men, I'd say. Like to talk things over?"

"No, but I'm thankful, all the same. I'm just roaming these days."

"Good for you. I know how it is. Wish I'd done a little roaming in my younger days."

When we said goodbye to each other, I almost called him Cousin. He had the eyes of a Shilling to me, but I'd never heard of any Shillings living near Gray.

We were heading in the general direction of South Sanford, the last town in Maine before New Hampshire. I didn't know when we would reach there. It was apparent already that there wouldn't be any sense in trying to keep up with a timetable, because we couldn't guess about unexpected delays up ahead.

One of those delays happened within the hour. A small pickup truck passed us and then stopped. The man driving it got out and waited for us to approach. "I passed you earlier, going the other way," he explained. "Been thinking about you ever since. Where are you going?"

"A far piece."

He took a folded envelope from a pocket and handed it to me, along with a ballpoint pen. "Would you mind signing this for me? I'd like your autograph."

He looked like a rational man and he seemed to be serious. "Why would you want my autograph?" I asked.

"I have a hunch that either you're a famous person or you will be a famous person."

"I'm not Greta Garbo," I told him, as I signed my name. It's too bad Uncle Waldo wasn't here. Whenever I'd get uppity about something, he used to tell me that I wasn't Greta Garbo. It was a family joke.

As we talked there, a big truck pulled off to the side. The driver wanted my autograph, too. "For my wife," he explained. "She collects."

"But how do you know she'll want mine?"

"Fate," he said. "Something told me to stop."

I wrote my name on the back of a blank check for him, and he handed me a dollar. I didn't want to accept it, but he insisted. People with the shorts are more sensitive about accepting things than people with plenty. Finally, I did take it, because he said it was a lucky dollar and I would need some luck on my journey.

"Was it a lucky dollar for you?" I asked.

"Sure. I have your autograph."

When the truck drove off, Tarzan tried to set too fast a pace. I slowed him down and told him, "It's a long time 'til night. Now mind your manners and show a little more respect. There's been a change in your cargo up here. Now you're carrying a celebrity. Ask any truck driver."

Maine is a state of fresh water. Its lakes, rivers, ponds and streams contain infinite billions of gallons, but Tarzan and I couldn't find a drop of it on our march. We must have taken

20

the driest route in New England. Even Depeche Toi, who had found a few little drinks in culverts, was thirsty by late afternoon. I wasn't carrying any water then. Didn't think it was necessary, and there wasn't any extra room on the horse for a jug.

Night wasn't far off when we turned into a farmyard. It was my intention to ask for water and for permission to sleep in the barn, but the farmer and his wife had other ideas. They invited me to supper, and I slept on a cot in the kitchen that night with the dog curled up on a blanket alongside. Tarzan spent the night with some steers, eating their hay and grain and saving his own.

I knew from my hosts' talk that they weren't Maine natives. He was a Harvard graduate and a former lawyer who had always wanted to farm and now he was doing it. His wife was a nice lady. She had a Boston accent, too.

I must have supplied most of the supper conversation. Found them easy to talk to and good listeners, the type who never interrupt. Practical people, too. Big barns but a small house, which was why the only space for me was in the kitchen.

That night, as the man set up the cot for me, he started joking about goals. "Your goal is to reach California," he said, "but what about your horse and your dog?"

"Same as mine."

"No, you are all individuals, and each of you should have your own goal. Where did you say you bought Tarzan?"

"I didn't, but from a riding academy near Portland. They picked him up from a nearby summer camp."

"In such case," he said, sounding like a lawyer, "it's highly probable that he is accustomed to salt water. Thus we can assume that he has waded in the Atlantic Ocean."

"We don't have to assume it," I told him. "I know the summer people rode him along the beaches. He's been in the ocean and he's not afraid of waves."

"Fine. Then Tarzan's goal should be to wash his feet in the Pacific Ocean. I daresay that no horse in history has ever

21

walked from the Atlantic to the Pacific and washed his feet in both. Now, what about the dog?"

"He's never been in the Atlantic, but I think he already has a goal in mind," I said, remembering how active he'd been the past two days. "Depeche Toi wants to be the first dog in history to visit every bush, tree and telephone pole in America, from coast to coast."

So when we went to sleep that night, the three of us were well fed, and each of us had a goal.

They really took farming seriously. Up early and breakfast on the stove by six-thirty. The farm had plenty of hens, and I enjoyed my first eggs since leaving the hospital. Depeche Toi had made a big hit, and he was fed a plate of scrambled eggs, too. The eggs were the first he'd ever had, but he didn't question them. He wolfed them down and licked the plate clean.

The farmer helped me pack Tarzan, and we were on our way before eight. Eleven, uneventful hours later, it seemed about time to call it a day. We had covered thirty miles and all of us were weary, Depeche Toi most of all. Traffic had been light, so I had let him run free. I suppose he'd run a hundred miles or so.

It was a clear, cold night and I knew it would get even colder. We were out of the wooded hills and in flat country, where northwest winds really bite. It was not a night for camping out. I started looking for a barn.

I tried two places. At the first, an elderly woman seemed just about to give us permission to use her barn. Then a younger woman, about my age, came out of the house and told her senior, "You mustn't! What will your son say when he comes home?" I found out later it was a case of 'hanging pants on the line,' for that family didn't have a man.

I stopped at a big house next, but the woman living there explained that she didn't have room for me. She'd closed off

22

all but two of her rooms for the winter. A true New England habit that keeps the heat bill low.

"What I had in mind was sleeping in your barn with my horse," I told her.

"I cannot permit that. A lady should never sleep in a barn!"

"Is there anyone on this road who might let me use his barn?"

"I don't think so. In these parts, we feel that barns are not for people. Why don't you camp in one of my fields? Just go in the fourth gate down the road. There's a little stream in that field, and a grove of gray birch at one end."

We found the field, and as we went through the gate, Tarzan lifted his head high and sent out a good whinny. A horse uses the whinny as a welcome, but there were no other horses in that field, so I don't know just what Tarzan was welcoming, unless it was the chance to rest.

Once freed of his saddle and cargo, the horse rolled over and over on the ground. His back itched after eleven hours under that load. I fed him, put two blankets on him, and set out extra hay and grain. Then I fixed food for the dog and myself. I had to awaken the dog from a sound sleep, but it didn't take him long to fall asleep again after he'd eaten. I rolled up in a blanket and followed his example.

Depeche Toi's growls awakened me. I sat up, grabbed his collar and looked around. A big, electric lantern was bobbing our way, and then a flashlight's beam was on me.

"Keep holding that dog," came a man's voice. "We're officers of the law."

The dog growled some more. He didn't believe them, and neither did I. "We have permission from the owner to camp here," I told him. "If you two are officers, where are your badges?"

"Under cover, and that's where you should be right now, too."

The woman who didn't believe that barns were for ladies had decided the same about fields. She had phoned the sheriff, and he had found a room for me in the nearby town. Tarzan had been invited back to her barn.

So all of us enjoyed shelter on that cold night. At one in the morning, the sheriff drove me to a small, private hospital that was run by a doctor and his wife. They were up waiting for me, although the doctor wasn't really up—he was flat on his back, as he had been for twenty years—paralyzed. His wife wheeled him about on a special contraption. He was still practicing, still helping people. A wonderful man.

His wife drove me back to Tarzan's barn the next morning. While the horse ate his grain, she and I talked. It was pleasant conversation, but I sensed that she was trying to tell me something and didn't know quite how to go about it. So I tried to make it easy for her by saying, "Some people don't approve of what I'm trying to do."

"My husband and I approve," she said.

"Thank you."

"And we wish you would change your mind."

I wasn't sure that I'd heard correctly. Depeche Toi was sitting there, head cocked and looking at her, as if he was puzzled, too.

"While you and I were having breakfast this morning, my husband phoned Minot," she continued. "He talked to your doctor there. So now we know about you, too." She paused, then added, "Courage isn't everything. It's just one thing."

I nodded and waited for her to say more, but she didn't. I was grateful for her concern, and pleased that she didn't press the issue. She was just reminding me of the time limit on my life, if I lived "restfully." I came close to telling her my secret: I had the Lord's approval. Or was it His blessing? Four-out-of-five was stronger than three-out-of-five.

Now I said, "I'm feeling better than I have in years. The fresh air helps some, I suppose, but the nice people I'm meeting along the way helps more."

She smiled, then put her hands on my shoulders and looked right into my eyes. "You'll get there, you *must* get there," she said. Then she kissed me on the left cheek, turned and

24

walked to her car and drove off. I don't think she looked back, but I waved goodbye anyway.

I meant to send her a thank-you postcard from the next big town, which was Sanford, but we strayed along the way—taking side roads to avoid traffic—and things were shut tight when we got there. Sanford has a trotting track, and the night caretaker there let me put Tarzan up in a box stall. I intended to share the stall, but instead I had a bed. The caretaker's wife wasn't well, and he wanted to go home, but he had to stay at the track because a horse was being trucked back from Lewiston. When I offered to take care of the horse and told him to go home, he thanked me and said I could have his bed for the night, or what was left of the night. The horse, a beautiful black stallion, arrived about midnight. The mattress I slept on was beautiful, too.

For a very special reason, I had planned on an early start the next morning. But by the time I'd packed Tarzan, Depeche Toi was missing. When the dog didn't answer my call, I went hunting for him. I suspected I'd find him playing with cats, and that's exactly what he was doing—two horse-barns away. Depeche Toi liked cats when he was a pup, and he never changed. Most cats seemed to know he was their friend.

I put the dog on lead again just to make sure he'd leave the track and his new friends. A few miles up the road, I left my companion outside while I went inside a restaurant and had a good, hot breakfast. That was my special reason for leaving early, and it was the first money I spent on my journey. It being a very cold day, every penny spent was well worth the value received.

Then we began our longest day thus far on the road. South Lebanon was our goal, but by early afternoon I figured we wouldn't make it, and by nightfall I was sure. We plodded right along until we came to a village, and in the darkness I didn't see a single farm. Two men standing in front of a closed store told me how to get to a farm up a dirt road. They said the place had a big, empty barn.

25

We found the farm all right, but the owner refused to let us use his barn. I offered to pay something, but he still said no. "I just can't risk it," he said. "You go on up this road. There are other farms with barns. They'll take care of you."

In the next two hours or so, seven farmers turned me away. I'm not going to identify that village, because its farmers weren't typical of Maine. Coldest Maine folks I'd ever run across.

We wasted time and nine extra miles that night. Finally, we went back to the original farm. The house was dark, but I kept hollering until an upstairs light went on and the owner stuck his head out the window and asked what was wrong.

"Not a blessed thing," I informed him, "except that we've been on the road for fourteen hours, it's cold out here, it's sleeting, and I have to find shelter for my animals!"

"Oh, it's you again! Stay right where you are!"

He sounded irritated, but he was pleasant enough when he came out of the house. "We'll put your horse and dog in the barn," he said, "and then I'll drive you to South Sanford. If it wasn't so late, I'd phone friends and find a place for you around here."

On the seven-mile drive to South Sanford, I asked if he was taking me to a hotel.

"Police station," he told me. "You can sleep there. I phoned and you're expected. I'll pick you up there in the morning and drive you back to my place. Do you mind sleeping in a police station?"

"I don't care where I sleep, so long as it's dry. But why couldn't I have stayed in your barn?"

"Too risky. I'm a mail route man. A Government man, you see, and I can't afford a scandal. You know how people gossip."

For fear that he might drive the car off the road, I didn't risk telling him that his passenger had been born in a jail. Back in the great year of 1891, my parents were living in the Water Falls section of Poland, Maine. Fire had destroyed the regular jail, and two rooms of our house were converted into

26

temporary cells, with barred windows and doors. Mama carried the keys, Papa brought the food to the guests, who were mostly tramps, and Grandpa's dog, a bloodhound-mastiff mixture, was the guard. When the Poland Town Hall burned, all the birth records did, too, but not mine. I never had an official birth certificate: Maine didn't start keeping records until eighteen days after I was born. Water Falls is now a part of Mechanic Falls, but that doesn't change the fact that I was never born officially. However, I did get here, and I did start my life in jail.

So the prospect of spending the night in a police station didn't bother me. I would be right back where I'd started, so to speak.

The police in South Sanford were very accommodating. They gave me a comfortable bed and I slept behind an unlocked door. I had a room, but there was a drunk in what they called a cage, and as we passed by he asked, "Are you in for being drunk, too?"

"No, I'm in for being sober."

"Proves my point!" he shouted. "It's senseless to stop drinking!"

I signed out early the next morning. The officers told me I didn't have to sign the police register, but I did. I wanted them to know I was leaving so they wouldn't worry about me.

Sure enough, the mail route man was waiting for me outside the police station. We returned to his house, and there his sister prepared a big breakfast for me and then gave me a nice lunch to carry. Since the sister lived there, it seemed strange to me that her brother had worried about me sleeping in the barn.

Tarzan, Depeche Toi and I were back on the road at nine. We were about twenty miles from South Lebanon, and I figured we'd pass through there and be well into New Hampshire by nightfall.

The prospects of that started fading within the hour. A car passed us and stopped, and out hopped two men and a woman. They said they were reporters from a paper in Portland, and that they'd run across my story at the police station in South Sanford. The three of them asked all sorts of questions, and I answered all those that I thought weren't too personal. Finally I told them that the talking wasn't getting me any closer to California. They laughed, asked a few more questions, and then we parted.

I was a little fussed, because we'd wasted almost an hour and any more delays would mean that we wouldn't reach New Hampshire. Somehow I felt that we wouldn't really be on our way until we'd left Maine behind us. Once over the line, our journey would become official. The thought never crossed my mind that the hour of talk there on Route 202 had been a lucky break for me.

About four that afternoon, a sign told us that South Lebanon, our last town in Maine, was three miles ahead. We'd covered about half that distance when a car coming toward us slowed down, then stopped. A man with a camera in his hand got out of the car. Depeche Toi ran up to him, and the man took his picture. Then he pointed his camera at Tarzan and me. As he came alongside, he said, "I'm from the Associated Press in Boston. Do you mind if I ask a few questions?"

He was very polite. We talked for a bit, and then I told him that I just had to get moving. I wasn't about to waste another hour. "I plan on making New Hampshire tonight," I explained.

"I don't want to hold you up, but we'd like some shots of you unpacking Tarzan, and of you feeding him and your dog. I've already made arrangements for the three of you to spend the night in South Lebanon, and a restaurant there will give you supper and breakfast."

It worked out just that way. The dog and I stayed in a private home that night, and Tarzan rested in a box stall. The restaurant owner told me to order anything I wanted. For supper, I ordered the lowest-priced things on the menu.

I didn't understand then that the meals were free. But I knew it the next morning, and breakfast was more on the expensive side.

An elderly lady, ninety or so, helped me pack Tarzan that morning. She had packed horses in the West in her younger days, and she taught me some tricks about where to place things and how to tie them, and she suggested some equipment that would come in handy.

About twenty people were there to see me off, and I think every one of them asked for my autograph. They were pleasant and neighborly. Real Maine people.

The New Hampshire border was a short distance away, but every step was sentimental to me. I hadn't been out of my beloved Maine for forty years, and I'd spent two years as a little girl in New Hampshire. I was leaving home, and in a way I was returning home.

On a direct line, we were about seventy miles from Minot. It had taken us six full days to reach the border. We weren't crows.

3   🐻   NEW HAMPSHIRE—MASSACHUSETTS

When I was four, Papa moved us to Jackson, New Hampshire. I don't recall why, except that he was a great one for changing jobs. We lived in a few other towns, too, before returning to Maine. Mama used to tell how I cried for a week about that, because I had to leave my best friend.

He was a tame bear and belonged to a neighbor. I called him Big Dog. He'd been raised from a cub and was as gentle as a pet dog, and stood taller than a man when upright. I loved that bear and he loved me, but Mama was relieved when we moved away. She was always afraid that the bear would cuff me.

Now I was revisiting my second favorite state: New Hampshire. Wherever we went in the Granite State, I found my luck in bloom. The time spent with those reporters from Portland and Boston had not been wasted. People knew about us and went out of their way to be pleasant and helpful. If there was a single crank in the whole state, they kept him hidden.

All along our route through New Hampshire, complete strangers invited us to spend the night with them. We could have spent months in that state alone, and there were times when it seemed that we would. It wasn't a question of a delay here and there, but of one delay after the other, and all of the delays were based on kindness.

Because of the many stops, it was a seldom day when we reached our planned destination before nightfall. Darkness comes early in the winter months, and that increased the dangers for us on the highways. By then I'd acquired a miner's light that faced backwards, but there was no guarantee that every driver would see it.

The police felt that way, too. If I was still short of my goal when darkness came, they'd drive out to meet me and provide an escort. Or if I was too far from my goal, they'd find a nearby place for us to stay. They kept a check on me all through the state, and that was one reason why I stuck to highways and not dirt roads. It helped them find me. Dirt roads would have made it easier for Tarzan, but in the long run they meant too many extra miles of travel.

Our first day in the Granite State ended ten miles short of Rochester, where a farmer had invited us to spend the night. They kept heaping my plate at supper, and I felt stuffed by the time the hot apple pie was served. I finished one piece out of politeness but declined more. Then we sat around the kitchen table talking and watching Depeche Toi enjoy his supper of meat scraps and boiled carrots.

"This isn't right," the farmer said. Then he turned to his boy, who was about ten, and told him, "Go down to the barn and bring back Tarzan and a half pail of oats."

I couldn't figure what the man had in mind, but his son did. The boy ran out of the house, and the farmer pushed a side table up to a window. When the boy returned with Tarzan and the oat pail, the pail went on the table, and the window was opened. The horse remained outside, but he stuck his head through the window and had his supper of oats.

A Maine farmer wouldn't think of doing a thing like that. As I was to learn, customs vary from state to state.

31

I slept in a double bed that night. Depeche Toi started the night on the floor, but he was curled up next to my head when I awakened in the morning. He wasn't shedding, and nobody else ever knew.

I was just about to saddle Tarzan when a big car drove into the yard. The three men in it said they'd been looking for me all night. They were from a television network and had a movie camera with them. First one I'd ever seen. They set it up on one of those old-fashioned tripods and then ran a line from it to the car battery.

"Just go right ahead saddling and packing," one man said. So I did, and I was still working away when he said, "Thanks very much. We'll run along now, but we'll be seeing you."

We kept running into them for the next couple of hours. They took pictures from both sides of the road, and once from the top of their car as they drove by. At one place, they asked me to ride Tarzan up a bank and onto a front lawn. When I obliged, a beautiful lady came out of the house with a tray of snacks for the dog, the horse and me. It might have been another state custom, but I think she knew we were coming, because it happened so fast.

The television men gave me a little money to buy hay for Tarzan and food for the dog, and that was the last we saw of them.

We got back on the road for Rochester, which was still four miles up ahead. Most of the traffic that morning was headed in our direction, so we stayed far off to the side and progress was slow. Then a horse van came along and stopped. The driver got out of it and said, "We're having a parade in Rochester, and the mayor sent me out to pick you up. He wants you to lead the parade."

Well, I just had to refuse. I wasn't dressed for any parade. In my getup, I was even worse than The Horribles, those awful clowns who used to make up the end of the parade back home on the Fourth of July. And, of course, I didn't know how Tarzan would behave in a parade.

So the horse van went off and again we headed for Rochester. I thought the parade would be over by the time we arrived, but it hadn't even started. It was waiting for me. Mayors don't discourage easily in New Hampshire.

Some parade officials placed us up front of the band and gave us a Boy Scout escort. A dozen motorcycle policemen roared past, the music started, and people cheered. I don't recall why they were having a parade in November, but I felt the way Lindbergh must have felt when he came home from Paris, and I know I looked like Buffalo Bill's wife. The people along the way shouted my name and waved, and I waved to them. Depeche Toi dashed from one side of the road to the other, saying hello to as many onlookers as possible.

It may have been the slowest parade in history. I just couldn't make Tarzan hurry, and every once in a while he'd come to a complete stop. The Boy Scouts were out of step and the band came close to bumping into us.

Finally, we reached the fairgrounds. There the parade ended and Tarzan was given a good stall for the night. Two of the Boy Scouts took me to their home as their good deed for the day. The dog was invited, too, and that night only Tarzan missed seeing the three of us on the television news.

"All over America tonight, millions of people must be watching you," said the father of the family. "You must feel thrilled."

"The only feeling I have right now is one of relief," I told him. "Watching us go up that steep bank to the front lawn, I was afraid I was going to fall out of the saddle."

The only unfriendly member of that family was the cat. She kept her distance from Depeche Toi. But when I awakened in the morning, there she was, curled up next to the dog. He certainly had a way with cats.

Rochester was where the Maine truck driver's prediction came true. It seemed like the whole town wanted my autograph, and we didn't make a mile an hour all morning long. It was there that I learned Tarzan was a trick horse. Children would ask him, "What do you do when you meet a lady?" and up would come his front right foot. On "What about a left-handed lady?" up would come his left foot. I imagine he was taught right and left at the summer camp, unless Depeche Toi taught him on the quiet.

Our next port of call was Manchester. When we reached there just before dark, we were surrounded by a crowd just coming from a church service. I was autographing away when the parish priest stepped up and gave me a ten-dollar bill. Then he gave me a Saint Christopher medal and his blessing. He didn't even ask about my religion, which was different than his. I regarded the priest as an agent of the Lord, and He was letting me know that four-out-of-five was indeed a blessing.

"This gentleman is Mr. Adams," said the priest.

Mr. Adams reached up and shook hands with me before saying, "You're dining with us and spending the night. If you'll be kind enough to dismount, my wife will drive you home and I'll lead Tarzan to the stable."

It turned out to be a two-night stop. "The horse needs a rest," Mr. Adams said at breakfast the next morning.

"And you need a vacation," said his wife. "Why, what's wrong?"

Suddenly, I was all choked up. I couldn't pull myself together and explain for a minute or so. They were worried and so was Depeche Toi. He tried to climb into my lap.

"I'm not unhappy," I managed to say. "When you said 'vacation', it was like pulling the plug out of the vinegar barrel. You see, this trip is my vacation."

"We understand," said Mr. Adams, but I knew that wasn't possible. They didn't ask any questions. They were polite folks. I wouldn't have told them the whole truth anyway: In all my years, I'd never had a single day of vacation. This trip was a trip, yes, but it was also my first vacation. It was as if I'd been saving up days for almost sixty-three years, but not knowing it.

They told me that I was their boss for the day, and asked what I'd like to do or see. Well, now that I'd been on television, I thought it was about time to see the inside of a tele-

34

vision studio. Mr. Adams telephoned a friend, and that afternoon I found myself sitting inside a studio and talking to a nice young lady. She was very interested in what I'd seen along the road from Minot, and asked all sorts of questions. So I gabbed away as if I hadn't talked for weeks. Then I happened to glance across the room and there was my big nose in the middle of a television monitor. "Are we on the air?" I asked. When she nodded, I swallowed hard. Too hard. I lost my power of speech almost, and couldn't say more than yes or no from then on.

That was quite a day in Manchester. Everywhere I went, people wanted autographs and some took my picture. While I was absent, others dropped by the Adams' house with gifts for me. I can't recall all the gifts, but they included a heavy shirt for me, army rations that would come in handy later on, a short leash and a blanket and dog food for Depeche Toi, and a waterproof blanket for Tarzan. A man from a big grain and food company called to say that I could draw supplies for Tarzan from any of the company's stores and grain elevators. That meant I wouldn't always have to carry food for the horse.

I couldn't accept everything that was offered, and it was a pity that I had to refuse some silk night clothes. I'd heard about how comfortable those silk things were, but they seemed inappropriate for the road.

The solid day of rest seemed to put fire into Tarzan's legs. He was all for hurrying and tossed his head in irritation when we stopped to give autographs. The dog had covered every square foot of Manchester, so he hadn't rested, but he did seem friskier than ever. As for myself, I felt a touch friskier and worried less about the rest of our journey. Unless New Englanders were absolutely different than other folks, my fellow Americans were wonderful people.

All through the rest of New Hampshire, reporters from newspapers stopped us and asked questions. Many of the questions had nothing to do with our journey: What did I think about Senator McCarthy, how did I feel about the space race, or did I think the Administration was doing enough to halt inflation? "Time will tell" was all I'd say. I didn't want to be controversial.

I didn't know what was going on in the world anyway. I hadn't seen a daily paper in years, and hadn't read a farm journal in months.

Not a one of those reporters asked me how I felt about winter. I could have told them that it was weeks away on the calendar, but already in my bones. So while we'd had a fine time in New Hampshire, I wasn't unhappy when our trail dipped southward into Massachusetts. We were inching our way closer to the promise of warmer days. Miles are miles, but on a map they are inches.

From where we crossed the line into the Bay State, a car could have made the round trip to Minot in less than a day without breaking the speed limits. We had been on the road almost two weeks.

I had an uneasy feeling about Massachusetts. I told Tarzan and the dog to watch their manners and I'd watch mine, although if we got into trouble it would be because of my pride and my big mouth. I didn't think I could sit by and just smile if anyone brought up the John Paul Jones subject.

The mast on his ship had come from one of the tallest pines in Maine, and my own kin had helped drive the oxen that hauled it to the ocean. That's a part of American history, but for a long time Massachusetts claimed that the tree came from there, and I'd heard there were still plenty of diehards around. I just had to hope that we wouldn't run into any of them.

It didn't seem like food would be much of a problem, and our cash position had grown to almost fifty dollars. It would have been more, except that I'd bought that hot breakfast and also a few straps to replace some of the pack string. I knew the remaining string wouldn't last forever, and I was hoping to find some discarded leather straps alongside the highways, tossed there from passing cars. I never did, but if I could have traded a hundred empty beer cans for one strap, why, I would have had more straps than I needed. Otherwise, we were in prime shape.

Traffic was light during the morning hours. Some of the people in passing cars waved, but none of the cars stopped. We were making good progress and putting the miles behind us. I should have been happy about that, but to tell the truth I started feeling sorry for myself. I wasn't Mary Pickford, but I'd grown fond of signing my autograph and talking to reporters.

We passed by a country store at noon, and a minute later I heard a man shouting. Tarzan pulled up of his own accord. I looked back and saw a man running our way. He was carrying a brown market bag as if it were a tray.

"I was waiting for you to come along," he said. "Some young folks, strangers to me, stopped an hour back and said you were on your way. They're passing the word along up ahead. How about some lunch?"

He had chocolate bars for me, carrots for Tarzan, and ground meat for Depeche Toi. "Have to get back and mind the store now. Oh, almost forgot. Here. Real Vermont cheese. Say hello to Betty for me when you get to California. Betty Grable."

The man laughed and hurried away. He forgot to mention his name and I still haven't met Betty Grable.

We were close to a town called Lunenburg, and somewhere on the outskirts a woman came running out of her house and asked if she could take our pictures. She was focusing her camera before I could say yes. So we posed for her, and then she asked if we'd had lunch.

"Just finished a chocolate bar lunch," I said.

"That's not nourishing enough. You need something hot on a day like this. Come along and get off that horse."

A stop wasn't on my mind just then, but something told me that I'd be a fool not to take lunch with the woman. Her name was Mrs. Jean Bryar, and while I didn't know it that day, she would be very important to my future. During lunch, she asked me all sorts of questions about my plans, and after lunch she showed me her kennel of sled dogs. They were Siberian Huskies and a similar, new breed called Alaskan Huskies. Mrs. Bryar raised and raced them and said they were quiet breeds, but those dogs went wild when they saw Depeche Toi, and he barked right back at them.

By the time we got underway again, the sky was overcast and the wind was coming from the northwest. Conditions spelled snow to me. I told Tarzan to walk a little faster. We were still fifteen miles short of the city where some people had invited us to spend the night, and snow wouldn't make the highway any safer.

An hour later, just as light snow started to fall, a car stopped up ahead. The driver walked back to us and asked where we were going. I told him.

"Too far and too dangerous," he said. "I live just around the bend. Take the first dirt road on the right and stop at the third house. I'll go ahead and tell my wife and get some hay down from the loft."

"Your wife won't mind?"

"Mind? Why she sent me out to find you. Now don't worry about the people who are expecting you. We'll phone them."

"I think I should push on."

"You'll be doing me a favor if you stay with us," he insisted. "I've been waiting since last Christmas to open a bottle of champagne, but my wife's been saving it for a special event. Your company would be the special event."

I couldn't turn him down, but I did turn down the champagne. He'd been waiting eleven months for a drink of champagne, and I'd waited over sixty years—and I'm still waiting. But Depeche Toi had a few licks. He didn't like it. Made him sneeze.

The family's name was Jones. I asked if they were related to John Paul Jones. They weren't.

"But I'll tell you something," said my host. "The mast of his ship came from a Maine pine tree, and an ancestor of mine helped fit it out. A great grandmother on my maternal side was a Stuart."

So we were cousins. I would meet many other fine people in Massachusetts, but I still remember him as the smartest man I'd met in that state.

On a couple of stormy nights in the Bay State, I considered forgetting my destination and staying over at a motel, but I hadn't seen any along the way that had shelter for horses. Swimming pools, yes, but never a little barn. And I didn't know then that most motels accept dogs. Also, I didn't know they'd let me in the way I was dressed. Prices scared me, too.

So I didn't try a motel or a hotel, and I didn't look twice at a fancy restaurant, no matter how hungry I was.

I was surprised one afternoon when the manager of a fashionable inn came running across the long lawn to the road and hailed us with, "We've been expecting you! This is the place!"

Tarzan stopped, just as if he knew we'd been expected, and I asked, "You sure this isn't a case of mistaken identity?"

The man laughed and explained that he'd phoned an invitation to us the night before. It was news to me, but he repeated it and we accepted. Tarzan went out back and had a meal of grain. Depeche Toi and I went into one of the fanciest dining rooms this side of a silent movie. The other diners were dressed like they were in the movies, too, but they all smiled at us.

A waiter gave me a menu and told me to order anything I liked. The manager stood there recommending things while I studied the list of impossible prices. I wanted to ask if the Maine lobster was solid gold. Finally, I asked for a bowl of soup. It was the cheapest thing I could find, and at two dollars it had to be good. Well, it was very good. I was ready to leave when two waiters came along with a full-course dinner for me, including the biggest steak I'd ever seen and a smaller one for Depeche Toi.

While we dined, other guests left their tables and came over to ours to ask questions or to give advice. One woman said she'd driven over our New Hampshire route and checked the day-by-day mileage. A man thought that Tarzan would be better off cantering, provided the hours were cut short.

What with eating and talking, it was a two-hour meal. A whole crowd went outside with me to meet Tarzan, and a young fellow of thirty or so showed me how to get better use from the pack straps. It was a long delay, but a pleasant one, and it made me think that Massachusetts people were going out of their way to be kind to me, even if they weren't asking for autographs.

Two days later I became very sure of their particular brand of kindness. It was the Sunday before Thanksgiving, and we were approaching a town that I'd planned to pass through hours earlier. A police car with two officers in it came along-side, and one of them said, "Where have you been? We've been looking for you all day. The whole town is waiting for you at Town Hall."

"I don't know anything about that."

"Then consider yourself under arrest. Just follow us."

The police car moved slowly, and we tagged along behind it. I knew I wasn't really under arrest, although I couldn't help remembering that the state had some peculiar, old blue laws.

Well, the whole town did seem to be waiting at Town Hall. And there, on the Sunday before Thanksgiving, all three of us enjoyed a real New England Thanksgiving dinner. Tarzan refused the turkey.

A little old lady told me that the turkey had been raised in Maine. "I saw to that myself," she said, "and also to the oysters in the stuffing. The oysters are from Maine, too." So was the squash in the pumpkin pie.

The Town Hall party lasted for hours. It was too late to move on, so we stayed overnight at the home of the lady who had found the Maine foods.

"Let us drink a toast to your future," she said at breakfast.

We raised our glasses of orange juice, clicked them, and downed the contents. She'd squeezed the juice from California oranges.

Springfield was our immediate destination. General Delivery there was the first forwarding address I'd given to a few folks back home in Maine. I didn't know if anyone would write me, but I was hoping.

If we could avoid delays, we could make it in two days. "And we'd better make it," I told Tarzan. "They're predicting the first big snow for tomorrow night, but from the looks of that sky it may come sooner."

We were heading up a hill when Tarzan whinnied and quickened his walk. His voice meant that he was saying hello to another horse, but I didn't see one around. Depeche Toi was up ahead. He barked, and then I saw three riders come over the crest of the hill. Two men and a woman.

"We're from the Brookfield Riding and Driving Club," the woman told me. "We came out to meet you and ride in with you to Mrs. Hamlett's in Spencer."

I thanked her and said that I was in a hurry to get to Springfield.

"The roads won't be passable by this time tomorrow," one of the men said. "Springfield will stay right where it is, but you're coming with us. Mrs. Hamlett won't hear of anything else. She wants you to have a real Thanksgiving."

"That's four days away," I objected.

"So it is, and you can use those four days and maybe more. How long have you had the cough?"

"It's not a real cough," I said. It had been with me two days, but it was no worse than when it had started.

"If that's not a real cough, then I'm not a real doctor. Now let's not debate any longer. We're all cold and Mrs. Hamlett has a fire going. Doctor's orders."

So we went to Spencer and became the guests of Mrs. Roland Hamlett, a warm-natured person who couldn't do enough for me and my horse and my dog. The snow arrived that night, and it lasted through the next two days. We stayed five days in all, right through Thanksgiving. A party-conscious town at that time of year, I'd say. One party after another, and the only ones I missed were the midnight suppers. My cough didn't worsen, but my side hurt and the doctor ordered me to bed at eleven each night. I didn't tell him about my lung. That might have spoiled everything. I told myself that the parties were restful affairs.

Depeche Toi stayed inside most of the time. He had a fine time playing with Mrs. Hamlett's cats. Meanwhile, Tarzan was well fed and dry in a neighbor's barn, where he enjoyed the society of other horses. A veterinarian looked over both of my friends and said they were in excellent condition.

When we took to the road for Springfield again, each of us carried Spencer hospitality with us. Depeche Toi had some boots, in case he ever needed them. Tarzan had a feed bag, but what he probably valued more were his new hard rubber shoes which took up a lot of the jar from the road. And I had a warm, gray coat as well as a poncho with a hood. Mrs. Hamlett thought I should have some silk night clothes, but I just couldn't see the sense in carrying things I wouldn't be using.

It wasn't supposed to snow the day we left Spencer, but it did, and we were invited to spend the night at an old inn where George Washington had once slept. Before we took to the road the next morning, the inn's owner painted a sign —TARZAN SLEPT HERE—and nailed it above my horse's box stall.

The roads were plowed and we made fair time. It was thirty miles to Springfield, and I was determined to make that city by nightfall. Then the snow arrived again. We couldn't see ten feet ahead, except when the wind blew. Depeche Toi stayed close, not wanting to lose us.

Tarzan walked along with his head down, and I just sat in the saddle, freezing, trying to figure out what to do. Any minute, I expected a truck to come along and run over us.

I just couldn't tell if we were on the side of the road or in the middle of it.

Something told me to get off the road. Tarzan slipped and almost lost his footing, and then the same something told me to dismount. I suppose that something was fright. I was scared, there was no doubt about that. I was freezing, but my courage was melting.

I dismounted and started leading Tarzan. His nose was on my back and he kept pushing me along. The wind was blowing right into my face. I kept telling the dog and the horse that everything would be all right soon, and that we'd find shelter.

Then He took a hand. The wind blew just the right way at just the right moment, and the timing enabled the driver of a car to see us. He stopped on the opposite side of the road and walked over to us.

"Going my way?" he asked.

"No. We're headed for Springfield."

"Thought so. I'm Mr. Coolidge from the Chamber of Commerce in Springfield. No, I'm not related to Calvin's family. A truck is coming along for the horse. You and the dog will ride with me."

Well, that's how we three got to Springfield. On wheels, and as guests of the Chamber of Commerce. Tarzan went to a stable, and the dog and I went to the Highland Hotel.

"The Highland is not our biggest hotel, but we consider it our best," Mr. Coolidge explained. "We feel you deserve only the best."

For fifty years, I'd carried the memory of a Boston hotel where I'd stayed overnight with my Grandpa. I'd remembered it as a palace, but the Boston place couldn't hold a candle to the Highland. My room had a full-length mirror, and what I saw in it made me feel pretty ridiculous. I sure looked like a hobo. For the first time on the journey, I wished I had been smart enough to pack a dress. Mr. Coolidge had told me that I was free to order anything I wanted in the dining room, but now I was too self-conscious to put in an appearance. Women hadn't worn trousers at the hotel in Boston when I was a girl, and times hadn't changed since. Coming through the lobby, I'd noticed that the other women guests wore skirts.

The telephone kept ringing away. I don't know why I didn't answer it, but I was used to party lines and perhaps I was waiting for my combination of rings. Anyway, I just stood by the window, looking down on the busy street, when a knock on the door sounded. I opened the door and found myself face to face with the hotel manager.

"I've been ringing you," he said. "The dining room will close in one hour. We've been expecting you."

I was frank. I told him I wasn't properly dressed.

"You are wrong, but I never argue with a lady," he told me. He went to the phone and talked to somebody, and a few seconds later a headwaiter, another waiter, and a cook arrived. I looked at the menu, and once again soup was the most inexpensive thing. So I ordered that. The men had different ideas about what I should order, but I stayed with soup.

Well, they brought my food right to my room and served me there. A dozen covered dishes at least. I didn't get any soup, but all of the food was delicious, and there was plenty left over for Depeche Toi.

I'd always known he was a smart dog, but he showed me something that night. The dog had never been in a hotel, and there we were, camped on the sixth floor. When he whined at the door, I'd open it for him, and out he'd go. He'd trot down the hallway to the elevators, and wait there for one to stop. Then he'd ride down to the lobby and go outdoors. Of course, the elevator men knew him, so on his return trip they'd let him off on the sixth floor. He always trotted up to the right door, which was mine, and scratched. He did that several times while we were at the Highland.

It was early to bed that night, and early to rise the next morning. I didn't want the hotel people going to all that trouble serving me in the room again, and I thought I could have breakfast in the dining room before any of the other guests arrived.

The plan worked for about five minutes. The dog and I were the only ones in the dining room, and then Mr. Coolidge and some reporters and cameramen descended on us. By the time others came to breakfast, I was the center of attraction. I didn't feel embarrassed because they were friendly.

Later, Mr. Coolidge drove me to the post office where they were holding two letters for me. The first was from a Mrs. Sawyer who wrote free-lance feature articles for the *Lewiston Journal's* Magazine Section. She thought that my trip would be a good subject for her, and she asked me to send her more information about myself, Tarzan and Depeche Toi. She'd planned to send along a letter to me from Governor Muskie of Maine introducing me to Governor Smiley of Idaho. I didn't know much about Idaho except that we'd argued some about potatoes, and I didn't know where Governor Smiley lived but I guessed I'd find him.

Her letter-writing began a friendship that lasted all through my trip, and is still growing.

Back at the hotel I phoned the writer of the other letter, Mrs. Bryar. She was the woman who raised sled dogs back in Lunenburg.

"I've been worried about you," she said. "I don't think you should try to find jobs along the way. Well, one of those pictures I took of you came out beautifully. I'm having it made into folders for you, and I'll send you a supply. You can autograph them and sell them. Are people still asking for your autograph?"

"Yes, but not in Massachusetts."

"Oh, those people just have to be conservative. Where will I send the folders?"

I stayed a second night at the Highland, and the next morning the Chamber of Commerce sent over a truck. Mr. Coolidge thought it would be safer if I didn't ride Tarzan in the city. The truck dropped us off in the outskirts and we started down the road to Connecticut. Banks of snow on all sides, but the road was clear and leading us south.

My cough had disappeared, and so had the hurt in my side. Very little traffic at that hour. It took us less time to cover the first mile than it had taken me to cross the lobby of the Highland for the last time where the manager and twenty guests wanted my autograph.

4 ☞ CONNECTICUT—NEW YORK

Connecticut was one surprise after another. Right from the start I met unusual people, types that I would never have known if I'd stayed in Minot.

There was the young fellow from New York City. I met him that first morning in the state, somewhere near Warehouse Point. He was having his car serviced as we passed by a gas station. He stepped right up and said, "Well, I'm in luck. I was on my way to Springfield to find you."

"We left there right after breakfast," I answered.

"I've come all the way from New York to talk to you. Do you have a minute?"

"Magazine man?"

"No, television. How about some coffee?"

There was a diner right next to the station. "Can't spend much time," I told him. "I want to make Windsor Locks by nightfall." I dismounted, hitched Tarzan to a pole and told the dog to stay put. Then we went into the diner and had coffee. The young man's name was Harry something. He gave me his card.

"Coffee enough?" he asked. "Would you like a steak or something else?"

"No, thanks. I eat light on the road for Tarzan's sake and save myself for supper."

"A good idea," said Harry, although I doubt that he got the point. "Tell me, are you sponsored?"

Now I didn't get his point, but I was frank and asked him what he meant. He showed me a newspaper clipping about a man who had just set off by bicycle to visit every state and get the signatures of all the Governors.

"This man is sponsored by a television show. They are paying him to do this in the hope of getting publicity for their show. But from all I've read, you don't seem to have a sponsor. You don't have a contract with anyone, right?"

"That's right, and I'm not about to agree to carry a television set across country, either. Tarzan is overloaded as it is."

Harry laughed and shook his head. "I'm here to invite you to be a guest on one of the big television shows." He named the show, which I'd heard about, and then he mentioned the sum that I'd be paid. The only reason my eyes didn't pop was that I didn't believe him. "We want to fit you into the show just before Christmas," he added.

"That's three weeks away," I said, "and all the money on earth can't keep me around here until then. I'll be down south by then or I'll be dead."

Harry argued a bit, but I wouldn't budge. When he left, he told me to telephone him collect if I changed my mind in the next few days.

The counterman shook his head and said, "I overheard. I wish I had a chance to grab that kind of money."

"You think he was serious?" I asked.

"He wasn't joking. But forget it. You never miss what you don't have, and that's a terrible program anyway. More coffee? On the house." As he poured, he said, "We hoped you'd come this way. The gas station has oats for Tarzan, I have meat for the dog, and that bag of sandwiches is for you. So who needs a million dollars?"

The offer hadn't amounted to that much, but it was a tidy

48

sum and it was apparently still there waiting for me. I don't know what they expected me to do for all that money, but I would have been willing to learn to sing and dance for it, except for the fact that I was in a hurry to beat out real winter. Also, just the thought of New York City had always scared me. There should be a limit to bigness.

Still, it was pleasant to think that somebody felt I had artistic talent, and the thinking helped warm me on the rest of the trip to Windsor Locks. I'd been invited to stay with the John Quidam family there. His two sons had driven to Springfield the day before to meet me and extend the invitation. They'd told me that even Tarzan would be welcome in the house, although the boy who had said it was smiling. "When you get there," the same boy told me, "just ask any policeman where we live. Here, I'll write my father's name on this paper for you."

When I found a policeman and asked for directions to the home, he shook his head and said he'd never heard of the name. Then he went into a drugstore to check in the telephone book. He was gone several minutes, and when he returned he was shaking his head again.

"There's no such family in Windsor Locks or any other town around here," he said. "I'm afraid you may be the victim of some kind of peculiar humor. The clerk in the store is Puerto Rican, and he says that Quidam means Nobody in Spanish. I'm sorry, but I don't think those boys were from Windsor Locks."

When I asked where the nearest stable was, he had better news for me: "I phoned a friend and he's on his way in for you with a truck. He has a barn and plenty of room for you and the dog."

The friend's name was Willard Dillon. Fifty that day, although he looked much younger to me. His wife was a year younger and she looked more like his daughter. They owned a big tobacco farm, but they were non-smokers, and they said that was the way to stay young-looking. I didn't tell them that I hadn't smoked for sixty-two years, and that I looked sixty-two when I became that. Maine climate might have had something to do with it.

We drove out to the tobacco farm in a two-horse van, and Tarzan spent the night in a Little Red Schoolhouse. Mr. Dillon's gramp had schooled in it during Civil War times, and when he became a man he bought it and moved it to the farm. The Dillon in between had changed it into a horse barn.

Roast goose was the big thing for supper that night. A big one, so I was afraid it would be tough, but it wasn't. "It's been roasting slow for ten hours," Mrs. Dillon said. "Willard loves goose, but I only give it to him on his birthday. So much trouble."

A young, tender goose wouldn't take so long to cook and would be plenty for two people. She hadn't thought of that, and thanked me.

I suppose I talked more that night than ever before or since. Seeing that little schoolhouse reminded me of the one I'd attended, and that's what got me going. My one-roomer had been painted red, too, and made from cedar slabs. That was back in 1899, when I was eight, and my folks moved ninety miles so I could start my education. There were eighteen others, ranging in age from me to twenty-two, and we were all studying different things. It was called an ungraded school. I went to that school for about five years, and then we moved to where there wasn't a school. Later, I attended a private academy in Portland, Maine, but about all they drummed into me there was that income is money coming in, and outgo is money spent, and if you make two columns and can add, you should know if you're going broke or getting rich.

Somehow, my talking about school days brought the conversation around to prayers. They couldn't recall the first ones they'd said, but I could recount my earliest one: "Please, God, help those that need Thy help, regardless of race, creed or color. As I'll pass this way but once, please lend me a guiding hand to help someone from out the ditch. I will not take Thy credit to myself." It was no trouble to remember, because my Papa made me learn that prayer when I was about four, and I've said it almost every night since. Except, of course, for the night in Minot weeks back when I suggested the tosses of the coin to the Lord.

Before we went to bed that night, Mr. Dillon advised me to detour around Hartford and not take the toll road. He got out a map and marked it for me, and showed me how the shortest route across the Hudson would be to head across the state to Danbury and then on into Brewster in New York State.

It was close to midnight, but that didn't stop him from phoning his mother in Farmington and making arrangements for us to spend the next night with her. By the time we reached his mother's house the following day, she'd phoned a friend twenty miles west of her for our next stop.

That's the way it went all across Connecticut. The older Mrs. Dillon was in her eighties, and so were all her friends. With one exception, all of them treated me as if I were a baby. They couldn't do enough for me or my boys.

I found the exception several nights later. She lived about a mile off Route 6 and not far from Waterbury. She was eighty-seven, widowed twice, and her third husband was seventy. She reminded me of my mother's old friend, Mrs. Williams, back in Minot.

"If this young man could take care of himself," she said, pointing to her husband, "I'd be tempted to join you."

"Go right ahead. I was a bachelor for sixty-six years. I can take care of myself."

"I've been thinking about it ever since I read about you in the papers. One is never too old for adventure. Would you mind if I went with you?"

I couldn't believe that she was serious. She didn't look like an outdoors woman, and she wasn't young. But she went right on talking as though her mind was made up:

"It may take several days for me to collect the proper equipment and buy a horse. And then you'll have to teach me how to ride. I've never been on a horse. Is it difficult?"

"It's easier flying off," her husband said.

She paid no attention to him, and went right on with "Hector likes your horse and your dog. He'll love going."

Hector was a breed of dog called Maltese. All of him was white fluff and he weighed about three pounds. He wore a tiny red ribbon between his ears. At first, Depeche Toi had thought he was a cat, but they got along fine together.

I had a time getting to sleep that night. One fool might make California, but I didn't know about two fools. I didn't want to be rude, but I didn't want to wait around for a month and teach her how to ride a horse. And if Hector ran around after Depeche Toi, the little thing would wear himself out in a day.

The husband wasn't present when we had breakfast the next morning. "He sleeps until noon every day," his wife explained. "He's on a special diet, and he won't eat at all unless I make him. So that's why I can't go with you. It's too bad. Wouldn't it be nice if he were strong enough to go with us?"

We were still only three when we got back on Route 6 and headed for Danbury. I had to pay attention to what we were doing that morning, for the road was uphill and down and full of curves, and there wasn't room for cars to pass each other. The road had been plowed but snow had drifted in since. Depeche Toi trotted just a few feet ahead, as he always did when he sensed there might be danger. So I wasn't doing any daydreaming.

There wasn't much traffic, but I kept an eye on every car that came along. That's how I happened to notice the same red car kept passing us. Heading our way, the driver always slowed down, and passing us from the rear he'd come on slow and swing wide of us. Coming and going, that car must have passed us a dozen times in one hour. The man behind the wheel acted as if he didn't know where he was going, but I waved my thanks to him anyway because he was being careful not to frighten Tarzan. Now that was considerate of him and I appreciated it. Most drivers think horses are machines.

Then a half hour or so passed by and I didn't see the red car. We turned into a parking space next to a little restaurant. There were trucks there, so I knew the food would be good and also good and cheap. On cold days, I favored a bowl of hot soup for lunch.

Inside, I sat next to a window where I could watch Tarzan and the dog. The soup was too thin, but it was hot, and I was enjoying it when along came the red car. It stopped, and the driver got out and strolled over to Tarzan. I remember that the man's face was tanned, and it seemed odd in the middle of all that snow.

From the way Depeche Toi greeted him, I could tell the man meant no harm to the horse. The dog could really wiggle when he liked a person. He had the looks and the coat of a pure Spaniel who'd been stretched, for his body was too long for his short legs, which was the Dachshund influence.

The man was still there when I finished my soup and went outside again. He was talking to Tarzan and didn't see me until I spoke. "He's not for sale," I said.

"Can't say that I blame you. He's a sound one. How old?"

"Aged, that's all I know."

"I know a little about horses. I'd say he was about fourteen. Do you really intend to ride him to California?"

"The Lord willing."

"You wouldn't have come this far if He wasn't," he said. "I've been waiting to meet you and get a good look at this horse. I've been offered ten-to-one odds that Tarzan won't make the coast."

"He'll make it unless we hear the Pacific has gone dry. He wants to wash his feet in it."

He laughed and said he'd read about that in a Florida newspaper. Then we chatted for awhile, and one thing that stuck in my mind was his suggestion that I get a pack horse. He thought the load might be too much for Tarzan in the mountain country out West. And he cautioned me against hurrying: "Take it easy, get there," was what his father had told him. It made sense to me.

Finally, he gave me his card and told me to telephone him and reverse the charges. "If Tarzan or you or the dog gets sick, and you can't find a veterinarian or a doctor, just pick up a phone and call my number. If I'm not there, the message will get to me. I'll get help to you, and it won't cost you a penny."

He had a foreign-sounding name. There was no address on his card, just a Waterbury telephone number. His card and his seemingly genuine interest in our welfare puzzled me a bit, but only until we reached Danbury. A state trooper was on the lookout for us there, and he showed us the way to the home where we'd been invited to spend the night. I told my story about the man in the red car and showed his card to the trooper.

"Of course he knows horses!" the trooper laughed. "One of the biggest gamblers in the East. Usually he's down at the Florida tracks this time of year. He's betting with somebody that Tarzan will make the coast, and you can be sure that it's not a small bet."

That night, I tore the card into little pieces and threw the pieces away. I wasn't about to encourage gambling. Uncle Waldo would have had a fit.

It was the last thing I wrote in my first diary. We'd been on the road four weeks, and all of the pages were filled.

Brewster, New York was our goal the next day. We were halfway there when a truck pulled to the side of the road ahead of us. The driver was a woman, and I judged her a bit older than myself.

"Heard on the radio that you were in Danbury last night,

and I figured you'd be coming along about now. I'd like to take you home for lunch and show you my horses. It's a bit out of your way. That's why I brought the truck."

Tarzan and Depeche Toi went into the truck, and we rode ten miles to the woman's home. She told me she'd been thirty-eight before she was on a horse for the first time, and even then she'd been lifted into the saddle, for she was crippled with arthritis in those days.

"I just decided to become a horse trainer, arthritis or no arthritis, and that's the way I started," she said. "I imagine it was just as sudden as your decision to go to California. Women are stronger-willed than men."

So she became a trainer of show horses and trick horses, and now the arthritis was gone. "Association with horses cured me. How else can you explain it?"

I couldn't, but I'd never given it any thought before. Well, she had some beautiful horses, and her favorite was a big bay gelding. He knew a particular trick that she thought I should teach Tarzan. "It could come in handy during your journey," she said. "It could save your life. Now watch."

She went up to this gelding and staggered around a bit, then asked him, "What would you do if I got drunk and could not get on you?" The horse nosed her from side to side to keep her going straight. They went along that way for a few feet, and then she fell down. Now the horse picked her up by one shoulder, held her on her feet, and then pushed her ahead.

"I had to wear a pad on the shoulder until he learned not to take hold too hard," she explained. "People underrate the intelligence of horses. You can teach a horse to do almost anything. Would you like me to teach this trick to Tarzan? You'd have to stay over for a few days."

I thanked her, but told her that we just couldn't spare the time. It was a good trick for anyone who owns a horse and intends to get drunk, but I wasn't planning on anything like that.

As she drove us back to the main road, she told me about a

horse farm on the far side of Brewster. "It's in Shrub Oak. You'll be welcome there. I'll phone ahead for you, or I'll drive you over there right now, if you like."

"I think we'd better walk," I told her. The way that woman drove, she must have taught her truck the trick of staying on the road. I figured she'd never get us to Shrub Oak in one piece.

Shrub Oak proved to be on the very far side of Brewster, and it was another day before we reached the horse farm. By then, a rear shoe of Tarzan's was loose, and I walked the last five miles.

They raised and trained hunters and jumpers there and sold them for fancy prices. We stayed there for two days, waiting for the nearest smithy to find the time to drive over and attend to Tarzan's shoe. While he was working on the shoe, I asked him if there were many horses in the area. The more I'd thought about it, the more the gambling man's suggestion about getting a pack horse appealed to me. I knew Tarzan wouldn't object.

"You'd be surprised at the horse population in this area," the smithy said. "Here we are, not more than fifty miles from New York City, and more and more horses every year. I could be working day and night."

"I was thinking about buying another horse to share the load. Just a walker, but used to traffic and saddle broke. He'd have to come cheap."

"There's an auction over near Peekskill tomorrow night and you'll find just what you want. I've seen some good horses sold there for as little as three or four hundred dollars."

"Thanks for the information. I'm headed for Peekskill anyway," I said, neglecting to add that I wouldn't bother to attend the auction. What with a little outgo here and there for necessities and soups, our funds were now under thirty dollars. I was willing to go as high as twenty dollars for a horse, but that was my limit.

By the time they'd held the auction, we'd passed by Peekskill and crossed the Hudson by means of Bear Mountain

Bridge. It was a toll bridge. Twenty-five cents for a car. "Your outfit doesn't have wheels, so you must be a walker," said the man at the gate. "Fifteen cents, please."

We turned south toward New Jersey. The road ran down the west bank of the Hudson, with the river on one side and high cliffs on the other. Signs warned about the danger of falling rocks.

It had been a long day for us. Forty miles, and a lot of them uphill and winding. That was three miles better than any previous day. We'd been averaging between seven and thirty-seven miles on travel days, depending on weather and delays.

The next town was called Stony Point, and that's where I'd planned to find shelter for the night. But we were still short of it by nightfall, and by then a light drizzle of rain had turned into sleet. The road was downhill and around sharp curves. I didn't dare ask Tarzan to hurry, for fear he'd slip.

He didn't, but a truck did. Just as we'd rounded a curve, the truck came up behind us. The sleet had made vision poor. The driver didn't notice my miner's light, and his headlights spotted us at the last moment. He slammed on his brakes and turned out from us, but as the rear of the truck skidded I felt some part of it bang into my left leg. Tarzan snorted and danced away, and for a few seconds I had my hands full.

The truck driver stopped and came back to us, and by flashlight we went over every inch of Tarzan. The horse didn't have a scratch. The driver apologized for scaring us so, but I didn't blame him for what had happened. He'd come along slowly, and the sleet was to blame. I was thankful that Tarzan and Depeche Toi were all right.

I climbed into the saddle and we started off again for Stony Point. I didn't think of my leg until it started to ache and pain. The biggest pain seemed to be just below the left knee.

Two cars raced by us, one after the other. Both were in the middle of the road, and chances were that the drivers didn't even see us. So I decided not to press our luck, and we turned in at the first big house showing lights. I wanted to phone the police and ask them to find me a place to stay.

It took about five minutes to convince the owner of the house that I wasn't a highwayman. If his wife hadn't seen my picture in the paper, he might have slammed the door in my face. As it was, they let me use the phone.

The officer said he'd send a police car out for me and also check on places for us to stay. "We heard you came over the bridge, and we've been looking for you for hours. Stay right where you are. The road is dangerous at night in this weather."

The horse and the dog stayed in the garage while we waited for the police. It took them almost two hours to arrive, and then it was another twenty minutes before the local feed store man came with his truck. The delay was caused by their difficulty in finding a place for me to stay, and then they awakened the feed man.

By midnight, Tarzan had been fed and was in a stall. Depeche Toi and I were in a heated, public garage. We climbed up into the cab of the biggest truck and went to sleep on the seat. We were too tired to even think of eating, and I was too worn to care about the pain in my leg.

It was the end of an eighteen-hour day.

The leg had less pain in it when we set off the next morning. It was a cold day, and the sleet had turned to snow. I thought of staying over and resting, but I was stiff from sleeping in that truck and didn't want a second night of the same.

Tarzan stayed reasonably dry. I had a blanket over him, and over that I put the waterproof canvas that the people back in Spencer, Massachusetts had given us.

Still, road conditions were such that I made it a short day. In mid-afternoon, we followed signs to a riding academy about a mile off the highway. There were plenty of empty stalls in the stable, and the owner was happy to rent me one for Tarzan, but he wouldn't hear of letting me sleep under the same roof. He did permit me to use an empty horse trailer out back. Then he gave me some advice:

"Never use a blanket on a horse, even in a storm like today. A horse stays healthy until you start pampering him. I guess you don't know much about horses."

I guess he'd never been to Maine. I didn't argue with him, and on his way home that night he drove me to a little restaurant a half mile away. I had supper there and then walked back to the stable. Putting my weight on the left leg didn't help it any. The pain increased.

Back at the stable, I said goodnight to Tarzan and retired to the trailer with Depeche Toi. The only thing wrong with the trailer was that it didn't have a door on the back. It was open to the coldest wind I'd ever known. So we went back to the stable and slept on hay in an otherwise empty stall. When the man came back the next morning, I was currying Tarzan.

"That was quite a wind last night. How did you sleep?"

"Never better," I told him. "I didn't ask you last night, but why didn't you let me sleep in here?"

"Insurance," he said. "If a horse dies I'm covered, but if a human dies, I might get into trouble."

"I wasn't planning on dying."

"You can't ever tell when you're going," he said. "I notice you're limping worse than last night."

He wasn't the most cheerful man I'd met. From his tone of voice, anyone would have thought I was dying.

He started measuring grain, then turned to me and said, "Not that I need the business, but I'd stay here at least another day. This looks like a two-day storm, and you don't look fit for travel. I can tell that the leg hurts you. Want me to phone for a doctor?"

"No. A day of rest and the leg will be as good as ever," I assured him. I said it loudly, hoping that the Lord would hear me, too, and see it my way. The leg was black and blue, and swollen from the knee to the ankle, and every time I stepped it really hurt. I was beginning to wonder if I hadn't been foolish in tearing up that gambling man's card.

Well, I didn't fool the stable owner. He had a little office in one corner, and he went in there and made a phone call. I didn't suspect anything until a half hour later when a Dr. Jenks arrived. He took a look at my leg and said I'd have to go to the hospital with him.

"How long will she be in?" asked my cheerful friend.

"Can't tell until I x-ray that leg."

The cheery one turned to me and asked if I wanted to put down a deposit against total charges.

"Now you listen to me, Don," said Dr. Jenks. "If you charge this lady one penny for boarding her horse, I'll have you run out of town. We are honored to have her in our midst. Now take special care of that horse."

Then we were on our way to the little hospital. Depeche Toi went with us, and they let him stay right with me for the two days they kept me in bed. X-rays proved that the shin bone hadn't been fractured, but the doctor said that medication and complete rest would have the leg in fair share in no time at all.

The swelling was down in twenty-four hours, and in another twenty-four most of the pain was gone. I had to argue some before Dr. Jenks would release me from the hospital.

"All right," he told me. "I'll let you go on your word of honor that you'll give that leg as much rest as possible for the next week."

"I'll tell you something. A person without legs wouldn't have trouble with Tarzan. When I'm in the saddle, both my legs are resting completely." He laughed, and I asked him what my bill ran to.

"It's been a pleasure to have you here," he said, "but I will have to charge you for the x-rays."

"Turn your back," I said. Then, as now, I kept my money in a secret place on my person. I'd never been robbed, but you never know. "You can look now. Here you are." I handed him a ten-dollar bill.

He took it and put it in his pocket. "There are some reporters waiting to talk to you downstairs," he said. "I'll ask one of them to drive you back to the stable. Good luck. I know you'll make California, all three of you."

"Thank you."

"You know, doctors aren't supposed to be superstitious, but I am. Thirteen is an unlucky number, and I wouldn't feel right charging you the full rate on this unlucky thirteenth day of December. Here's your change." He handed me three ten-dollar bills and said, "Happy Birthday." Then he walked out of the room. I never saw him again.

And I never figured out how he knew I'd been born on the thirteenth day of December in 1891.

5 🐎 NEW JERSEY—PENNSYLVANIA

So I'd just turned sixty-three when I climbed aboard Tarzan again. The stable owner said there'd be no charge, and his extra birthday gift to me was a supply of grain. He explained that he hadn't realized who I was when I'd first arrived.

His wife and daughter were there to meet me and now to see me off. The little girl asked for my autograph. I gave it to her and then asked for hers.

"I don't do this for everybody, but you're special," she said. She wrote her name down three times on the same piece of paper. "One for you, one for Tarzan, and one for the little doggy."

Then we headed down the road for New Jersey. Depeche Toi wore his blanket, Tarzan wore his waterproof one, and I had the poncho over my heavy, grey coat, with the hood over my head. It wasn't snowing, but it was still cold. A Newark paper ran a picture of us the next day. We looked like three visitors from outer space. It's a wonder we didn't frighten the children.

Not much else was happening in New Jersey that week. Some days we were stopped as many as six times by reporters.

They always apologized for delaying us, and they made a big thing out of the fact that I'd just "ridden into" my sixty-third year.

Most of the time we were on the East Coast Truck Road. It wasn't the most direct route for us, but it was the safest. The way those cars sped on, the highways weren't safe, even for cars. Trucks speed, too, of course, but those drivers know how to handle their vehicles.

Next to safety, the reason for taking that road was its nearness to riding academies. I was told that we'd never be more than ten miles from one, and that was a comforting thing to know in the stormy season.

We ran into a streak of luck all along that road. An hour or so before dusk every day, truckmen who passed us would notify the police in the town up ahead that we were on our way. By the time we pulled into that town, the police usually had accommodations ready and waiting for us. Sometimes I'd have supper alone in the cheapest restaurant I could find and other times I was the guest of the fanciest local restaurant. I was having a little trouble with my coughing again, and the first thing I asked for in the fancy places was a cup of hot coffee. This helped relieve the cough, and often it stimulated my appetite, and it never prevented me getting a good night's sleep.

We were averaging about eight hours a day on the road now, but not making the mileage we should have. Whenever reporters delayed us, people would gather and ask questions. You can eat up an hour pretty fast that way.

And then there were the truck drivers. Many times, a truck would stop and the driver would tell me just how to get through Missouri, or what I should see in Richmond, Virginia, or where I should eat in Kansas City. And sometimes the drivers would bring me invitations from people who wanted us to stay with them. Some of the invitations were from as far away as Texas, where we didn't intend to go.

By the fourth day in the state, I was beginning to think we'd been adopted by truck drivers. Those coming toward us often held up two fingers in the V sign invented by Mr. Churchill during the war.

Then I found out that we had, in a way, been adopted by at least one company. One of those huge moving vans stopped on the opposite side of the road. The lettering on the side said it belonged to a coast-to-coast moving company.

"How are you doing?" asked the driver.

"Fine," I said, and then I had a spell of coughing.

"Anything I can do for you?"

"Not unless you have a cup of hot coffee handy."

"Don't mind if I do," he said. "There's a place a quarter mile up ahead of you. I'll turn around and meet you there."

He was as good as his word. We sat at a table and he ordered two coffees. "All the drivers in my company have been ordered to keep an eye out for you," he explained. "The big boss wants us to lend you any assistance, anytime, anywhere. So don't hesitate to flag any of our vans."

After my third cup of coffee, I told him I didn't want to delay him any longer, but he said the glare from the snow was tough on his eyes. "Don't worry. The company didn't put a time limit on helping you."

Then a policeman walked into the restaurant.

"We expected you a couple of hours ago," he said. "Everybody is worried. They can't start the party without you. You ride on ahead. I'll drive at your rear and keep the headlights on you, so you'll be safe."

I didn't know what party I was going to, but I did want to get to the next town in safe fashion. So we started up the road with the police car crawling behind us.

The police took Tarzan and Depeche Toi to a stable, and then they drove me to the home of Maria and Michael Kuziak, a third generation Polish family. It was the night of December 19th.

I didn't know what all the excitement was about when I walked into the house. About twenty adults were there, all wearing funny paper hats and blowing away on toy horns. A birthday party for me!

There were five or six of those day-by-day calendars tacked to one wall. Every one of them read DECEMBER 13.

"You folks in New Jersey are a bit behind the rest of the world," I said. "Today is the 19th."

"We know, but you spent your real birthday in a hospital, and we wanted you to have a party."

Well, that was some party, complete with the biggest birthday cake I'd ever seen. I didn't count the candles, for fear I'd find more than sixty-three. And the birthday supper had foods I'd never tasted before. Back in Maine, I'd had French, Finn, Italian and Spanish neighbors, so I'd had some foreign foods, but Polish dishes were new to me. When I told Maria how good the food was, she promised me a surprise for breakfast.

There was another surprise first. We went to the garage, and inside I found Tarzan and Depeche Toi. Maria explained that the party was for them, also. The good people had gifts for my friends too, starting with pieces of birthday cake. Tarzan had grain with wine poured over it, a winter custom in Poland, I was told. My horse didn't complain. I opened a cardboard box for the dog, and inside it were three little kittens. Those people had read about his fondness for cats. It was a joke gift, of course. Nobody expected us to take the kittens on the road, which relieved me. They also had dried beef liver for the dog and a present for me: two pairs of warm, lined gloves.

I used up about a week of pages in my second diary that night. Those fine people, all strangers to me, had given me the finest birthday since my number four. That was in 1895, when my Grandpa Libby gave me a dark red Durham milking heifer. The bill of transfer, long since lost, read: "Payments of ten thousand kisses to be paid by installments. Delivered to my granddaughter Mesannie, in care of her mother. (Signed) George Libby." Not many four-year-old girls owned cows in those days.

Maria's breakfast surprise was another Polish dish: All the fried salt pork I could eat. It was brown and crisp, just the way Mama used to fix it. I didn't say anything to Maria, but I was thinking that somebody from Poland must have visited Maine centuries ago.

The Kuziaks wanted us to stay over with them for a few days, but I was planning to spend Christmas Day in Philadelphia. That city was still quite a piece down the road, and I was hoping to make it before the post office closed on Christmas Eve. Mail might be waiting for me there.

We covered twenty miles on that December 20th and ended up as guests of a town jail. The police couldn't find another place for us to stay, but at least it gave the reporters a chance to write something new about us. They took pictures of the jailer locking Depeche Toi and me in a cell. Then they spent quite a bit of time posing Tarzan so that he'd look like he was reading a road map. He kept trying to eat the map.

About ten that night, just as I was about ready to call it a day, a woman rushed into the jail. She'd heard about us over the radio and thought we'd been arrested and had come to rescue us. She'd driven her trailer from her home in White Horse, which was a good forty miles away in Pennsylvania.

Samantha Hollis was her name. She didn't like the Samantha and told me to call her Sam. She didn't like Mesannie, either. She called me Annie.

Sam told me that her husband's name was Bill, but he told me later that his name was Lawrence, but she had never liked Lawrence.

So that's how we got to Pennsylvania. Sam took us.

Even before meeting us, Sam and Bill Hollis had decided that we would spend Christmas week with them. I suspected that Sam did most of the deciding. When I told her I wanted to be in Philadelphia for Christmas, she said, "No. You want to be there on New Year's Eve. That's the only time to be in

66

Philadelphia. Besides, your animals need rest and so do you. Am I right, Bill?"

"Absolutely," said Bill, or Lawrence. In the six days we remained there, I never heard him disagree with Sam.

They were real animal lovers. Horses and ponies in the barn, and a house filled with all sorts of pets. The biggest house pet was a dog named Lady, and he was also the biggest dog I'd ever seen. Depeche Toi looked the size of a pup in comparison, and Lady licked him all over as if he were a pup. I thought Lady was an odd name for the big dog, and I said as much.

"He has a strong, maternal instinct," explained Sam. "He worries about the other pets."

The other pets were three monkeys, at least ten cats, a rabbit, some kind of black bird that could say a few swear words, and a banty-rooster. Some had been bought and some had been found, but in each case the pets had once been abused. The month before, Sam and Bill had bought a sick llama from a carnival man, but they hadn't been able to save the poor animal. "We don't like people who abuse animals," was the way Sam put it. "People can call the police for help, but animals can't."

I think she was really more concerned about my friends than me, and that's why she had rushed over to the jail. Not that she thought I was abusing my friends, but that my friends could use some rest. If that's the way it was with her, it was all right with me.

Except for the rabbit, Depeche Toi fit right in with the other pets. My dog's Dachshund blood excited him when he came close to the rabbit, so they weren't allowed to stay in the same room. I was surprised that he got along so well with the monkeys. Maybe he thought they were a new kind of people.

Next to rest and pleasant company, that Christmas stayover taught me something that was a big help through all the days to come. Bill Hollis was an efficiency expert. "I show companies how to lose money more efficiently," he told me.

One morning he had me packing and unpacking Tarzan. He watched the way I did things and made notes on a pad. The horse and Depeche Toi were two confused animals. Each time I packed, they thought we were headed for the road. I'd had the packing down to a system after almost two months on the road, and I could strap and tie everything aboard Tarzan in about fifty minutes.

That afternoon Bill weighed some of the gear and also cut up some old harnesses into different lengths of straps. Then he showed me just how to pack Tarzan, using only straps. No string at all. He was real clever in the way he used the loops on the breast collar to strap bed rolls up front.

"Do it this way, and you'll cut your time in half," he told me. "Nothing will slip now, and the weight is distributed as it should be, with sixty-five percent over the loins."

We may have looked much the same as before when we set off for Philadelphia after Christmas, but we were a much more efficient outfit. I could tell from the way Tarzan moved that he liked the new arrangement.

Bill had timed the packing in twenty-eight minutes, and with practice I knew I'd be able to cut down on that.

"From here on," he'd said, "you'll save at least two hundred and fifty minutes a week."

I didn't know what I'd do with the minutes saved, but I figured I'd find some way to spend them.

We reached Philadelphia on the last day of the year. I found a stable for Tarzan and the dog several miles from the heart of the city, but there was no place nearby for me. So I took an electric car into town, planning to check for any mail and then hunt up a room for the night.

A small, heavy package and about fifty letters were waiting for me. Most of the mail was addressed to me by name, but a few letters had been sent to "Lady Tramp on a Horse." And then there were a few postcards sent care of me to Tarzan and Depeche Toi.

I opened the package right there at the window. It contained one thousand folders from Mrs. Bryar, the woman who owned the sled dogs back in Massachusetts. The front of the folder carried a picture of Tarzan, Depeche Toi and myself. I looked a sight, but it was still the best picture I'd ever seen of myself. And on the inside of the folder was this poem:

> If you think you're beaten, you are;
> If you think you dare not, you don't.
> If you'd like to win but you think you can't,
> It's almost a cinch that you won't.
>
> If you think you'll lose, you're lost,
> For out of the world we find
> Success begins with a feliow's will—
> And it's all in the State of Mind.

I don't know who wrote the poem, but he had the right idea. When I showed it to the postal clerk, he said the poem should have a title.

"The printer forgot to put it in," I told him. "It's LIFE BEGINS AT 63." I don't know if he believed me or not, but he did ask if he could buy one of the folders. "That's the general idea," I said.

"And autograph it for me, please. My kids will get a kick out of this. How much?"

"Five cents," I told him. He gave me a quarter and told me to keep the change.

The fattest envelope was from Mrs. Sawyer. Inside it was another envelope addressed to Governor Smiley of Idaho from my Governor Muskie from Maine. This second envelope was unsealed, and an accompanying note gave me permission to read it. I didn't. I sealed the envelope without even peeking inside. I'd never read anybody else's mail and didn't intend to start.

After leaving the post office, I made the rounds of about six hotels trying to find a room and not doing so. The city was filled up for the big Mummer's Parade the next day. Nobody had warned me about that. I suppose Sam forgot.

69

Finally, a clerk in one hotel phoned around and located a room for me in a little, quiet place on a sidestreet. It was a big room with a private bath, and it took me about ten minutes to figure out the plumbing and get the hot water running. Then I soaked in the tub for a good hour.

Baths and laundry had been two of my worries when the journey began, but neither was ever a problem. When I stayed in homes, folks usually asked for my washing straight off. Other times, I did the washing myself or sent it out, and in such cases I was seldom charged.

Just before midnight, I walked to the center of the city to enjoy the excitement of New Year's Eve. It was crowded, and nobody recognized me. I suppose I just looked like another hobo.

I'd heard other women tell of the awful men they'd met on such occasions, but the only man who spoke to me was well dressed and drunk. He tried to hug me when he found out I was a woman, but he fell down while trying.

That was the only incident before midnight. The second one on that eve came about one in the morning when I wandered into the ladies' room in a railroad station. The attendant gave me sort of a peculiar look, but she didn't say anything.

A few minutes later, as I was walking out, I found myself surrounded by several large women in uniform. One asked for my name, and I told her.

She laughed and said, "Why then you're the lady who is riding her horse to California. Please forgive us. We were afraid you were somebody else."

The somebody else was a man who had dressed as a woman and used the ladies' room the week before. He was nude when he came out, and several women had fainted. So this time, the attendants suspected that I was the same man and would try the same thing again.

Quite a crowd had gathered around us while we chatted. It was too bad I'd left my folders back at the hotel.

I returned to the stable later that morning, and by noon we were working our way across the city. We were looking for a bridle path that would take us through a small park, then up a street to a big park to another bridle path that would take us to a police stable. It was quite some miles to that stable, and I was hoping for no delays, but now that I was on the horse everybody seemed to recognize me.

It was the first day of the new year, so when people asked how long we'd been on the road, I'd say, "This is our second year."

Thanks to the park police, we were able to make fair time in the parks. They were keeping an eye on us so that we could get to the stable before dark, but they couldn't keep people from stopping us on the city's streets, where they had no authority. We lost time on the streets, but otherwise we made a profit: I sold eighteen folders and made over three dollars.

It was dark by the time we reached the big park, and two mounted park policemen were there to escort us over the last few miles to the stable. I'd planned on spending just one night there, but the captain decided that Tarzan needed new shoes all around. That meant an extra night.

"Now don't fret," the captain told me. "We've reserved a room for you and the dog at the finest hotel in the city. As soon as you're through with the reporters, I'll take you there and we'll have a special dinner prepared by the finest chef in America."

Well, the "finest hotel" was his own home, and the "finest chef" was his wife. The supper, which is called a dinner in Philadelphia, was the finest I could recall. An orange duck, they called it, plus all the trimmings.

They owned two Persian cats, and the cats helped Depeche Toi eat his special supper of chopped meat and cooked string beans. He knew his place as a guest and didn't object to the cats.

When we left Philadelphia two days later, Tarzan owned

71

a real saddle blanket for the first time. That and his new shoes were gifts from the park police. And he also carried two first-grade, all-leather saddle bags, which were gifts from a lady whose son had brought them home from the first World War. A wide leather strap prevented them from chafing Tarzan's back. I fitted the bags as efficiently as possible, and stuffed them with my mail.

A town called Media was our next stop. There was a nice-looking inn there, and while I pondered whether we could afford it, the innkeeper came outside and extended an invitation. He'd just bought a horse, so he had the place and the feed for Tarzan.

The Lion's Club was dining at the inn that night, and the chairman asked me to be the club's special guest. I told him I was weary. Then when he told me they were having steak, I changed my mind about being weary.

After supper, the Lions took care of old and new business. The chairman introduced me and asked me to say a few words. I'd never made a speech in my life, but the gentlemen asked questions and got me started, and after that it was easy. I told them about how I'd bought Tarzan with pickle money, and about my coin-tossing agreement with the Lord, and about my life in Maine. They laughed and applauded every time I told them something new, and finally I was laughing so hard I couldn't continue.

Up until this experience, I'd always thought the life I'd lived was a pretty hard one. I'd never seen much fun in it, but here I was, in Media, laughing about it.

There was a lesson in it for me. I didn't know what it was. Uncle Waldo would have known, but he wasn't around to tell me.

All I knew was what I felt. When I climbed into bed that night, I felt happier than ever before.

Chadds Ford was only ten miles from Media, but they were the longest ten miles we covered in Pennsylvania. A man at the inn had told me about a dirt road shortcut. We found the road without any trouble, but it took us two days to find Chadds Ford.

That town had a big inn, too, although it seemed more like a hotel. Chadds Ford Inn, it was called, and Mr. Flaherty, the manager, invited us to stay there. Tarzan was put up in a stable that hadn't housed a horse in years.

After I signed the register, they showed me an older one. The last signature in it belonged to the man who rode horseback from California to the New York World's Fair in 1939. He still had some distance to go and had already worn out seven horses. That made me think Tarzan was a miracle horse. He looked fitter than when we'd started.

When I went out to saddle Tarzan the next morning, I found that he had company. A man was sitting there on a box and making a drawing of my horse.

"I hope you don't mind," he said. "I heard you were here and I wanted to make a head sketch of Tarzan. I'm almost finished." When I didn't say anything, he added, "My name is Andrew Wyeth. Mr. Flaherty knows me."

I looked over his shoulder as he worked, and I liked what I saw. I could tell that it was Tarzan, and not just any horse. "You're pretty good," I told him.

"Thank you," he said. He added a few lines to the drawing then stood up and thanked me again. I had to walk about ten feet to get the saddle, and when I turned around Mr. Wyeth was gone.

When we left the inn a half hour later, a light, wet snow was falling. It was slippery underfoot, and I made sure Tarzan kept to a slow walk. Cars made a swishing sound on the wet road as they passed us, and that always made Tarzan want to dance a bit.

The road brought us up a slight grade to the bridge that crossed the Brandywine, which is a river or a creek, depending upon the person talking about it. It was a two-lane paved road, with wire cables strung along the sides to keep cars from rolling over embankments. I had a fine view of Brandywine Battlefield Park where one of the great battles of the Revolutionary War was fought.

There wasn't much traffic as we started the climb to the bridge. Our outfit took up about half a lane, so drivers were careful not to pass one another when they saw us, which gave us plenty of room. I was able to pay strict attention to Tarzan.

We'd just crossed the bridge and started down the grade on the west side when I heard a horn tooting to our rear. I turned my head and saw two trucks. A small one was trying to pass a big one. It was a fool thing to try, for it left the big truck with no place to go except smack into Tarzan and me.

Thank the Lord, the driver of the big truck was wearing his thinking cap that morning. He feared his air brakes would scare Tarzan and send the horse over the bank, so he went into neutral, hoping to turn out and coast by us. Of course, he was also hoping the little truck would give him the room.

The close sounds to our rear—horn, swishing tires and motors—caused Tarzan to rear. He whirled and came down with his front feet over the wire cable. Then his hind feet slipped and we went down just as the big truck swerved out and missed us. It was so close that the driver thought he had hit us. He slammed on his brakes and skidded to a sideways stop up ahead. The truck blocked off both lanes.

The driver came running back to us, and he found me upside down and out cold. My feet were still in the stirrups.

The wire cable had held up Tarzan's front, and when his rear went down the saddle had slipped. I should have been thrown, but the sudden action had jammed my feet into the stirrups, and I had remained in the saddle, more or less. So I ended up under Tarzan's belly.

I was unconscious for only a few minutes. When I came to I was still on the road, Depeche Toi was licking my face, and two men were trying to free my feet. Because of the felt shoes and rubbers I wore, my feet were too big for those stirrups and I'd ride with just my toes sticking in. Now the too big feet were caught in too small stirrups.

Tarzan stood as nice as you please while the men freed my feet. By that time, quite a crowd had gathered, but the only familiar face I saw belonged to Mr. Flaherty.

"The only place you three are going today is back to the inn," he said.

I seemed to be in one piece, and so did Tarzan. Some of the men helped to unload him and put the gear into Mr. Flaherty's car. Then Tarzan started acting like a wild horse. I couldn't get a foot in the stirrup. I tried leading him, but he reared and lifted me like I was a feather.

So the dog and I rode back to Chadds Ford Inn in Mr. Flaherty's car. Tarzan was led back by the strongest man present.

I didn't have to be persuaded to lie down and rest for the balance of the daylight hours. My whole body ached, but it was a small price to pay for my incredible luck. I told myself that I was lucky to be alive, and that the accident had happened in the right place at the right time. I said a prayer at eleven that morning, and it included thanks to the man who had thought of putting those wire cables alongside the road.

I enjoyed lunch in bed. Then the doctor arrived. I'd asked for a vet to look Tarzan over. Mr. Flaherty had thought of the doctor for me.

"How do you feel?" this doctor asked.

"Well bruised," I told him. "Otherwise, I'm fine. I don't need a doctor."

"Judging from the report of the accident, you may need ten doctors. I'll take your pulse first." He did, and then he said, "I can tell you that you are not in a state of shock."

After that, he took my temperature and examined me. "Nothing broken, but you'll be stiff for days and sore for a week. All I can prescribe is plenty of rest."

"Doctors keep telling me that," I told him.

"And they always will. By the way, I've examined your horse. Nothing to worry about. A few small scratches and a little swell in a rear ankle. The bone isn't broken. Something hit him there. He can use some rest, too."

"Are you a doctor or a vet?"

"A little of both. I'll drop by tomorrow."

"I won't be here."

"You'll change your mind," he laughed, and he was right. The next morning I was so stiff and sore that all I wanted out of life was one hot bath after the other. I didn't budge from that room until nightfall, and then I was obliged to, having accepted a supper invitation from Mr. Wyeth, the man who did the drawing of Tarzan.

He had several other guests there. The supper was in my honor, although I didn't have to make a speech. Mr. Wyeth showed me a new drawing he made of Tarzan, with me in the saddle. I judged his picture of me as better than the one on the folder, and told him so. I also told him that his work was just as good as some professional artists who sold their drawings for fancy prices in Portland, Maine every summer. "You should try selling your stuff," I told him, and he promised to think about it.

When we started our journey again, all three of us went on foot. I wanted to lead Tarzan across the bridge, because he was limping a bit on that sore ankle. I was stiff, too, and thought that walking would work off the stiffness.

Once we were over the bridge, I kept right on walking. Tarzan was skitterish, and he nickered every time he saw a truck. His nervousness and limp didn't improve as the day moved on. So I stayed out of the saddle and walked all of the twelve miles to Kennet Square.

Tarzan's ankle wasn't swollen the next day, so I started out in the saddle. He didn't groan or grunt, but it didn't take long for me to know that the ankle still hurt him. It was the ankle on his right hind leg, and he kept moving over to keep the right foot on the soft shoulder of the road. Whenever we stopped, he stood on three legs and favored the hind one.

I found a veterinarian and he examined the ankle.

"No broken bones," the vet reported, "but this ankle will only get worse unless it has rest and warmth. Why are you in such a hurry to get to California?"

"I'm not. I'm just in a hurry to lose winter. I thought we'd beat the cold weather south, but here we are right in the middle of it."

"You've got tunnels and mountains ahead of you, and this horse's ankle will never make those mountains this time of year. Why don't you truck south?"

I told him that I didn't own a truck and that I didn't know of anybody who was about to give me one. Well, the upshot of our talk was that the vet telephoned a man who was in the business of transporting horses and the man was sending an empty van down near Lexington, Kentucky to pick up a load of horses. I was happy to hear that he had room for us, but not so happy to hear the price. Then the vet explained who we were, and the price was cut in half.

A day later, we started the drive for Kentucky. I sat up front in the cab and saw the rest of Pennsylvania and some of West Virginia. Tarzan and Depeche Toi were in the van and saw only each other.

We went through a series of tunnels that might have frightened the horse, and over some mountains that a healthy horse couldn't have crossed, even without a load. As it was, the van went around two of the mountains.

When we moved under our own steam again, we were in Kentucky and fifteen miles east of Lexington. We'd left the Maine kind of winter behind us, and that was worth every penny of the cost. And we were real tramps now: The three of us owned a dollar and nineteen cents.

6   🐎   KENTUCKY—TENNESSEE

The sun disappeared and the sky darkened long before we reached Lexington. "Get ready for some good old Kentucky rain," I told my friends.

What came was snow. We'd left winter behind us, but not for long. It didn't seem fair. We were in the South, now, and the weatherman didn't know what he was doing.

It snowed on and off all day. I walked when it came down and rode when it didn't. Tarzan had lost his limp, but I still had some of my stiffness, and my back was bothering me a little. I supposed that was because I'd hit the ground hard back at Chadds Ford. Thirty years before, a tree Uncle Waldo had cut the wrong way fell down my way. We'd had a collision, the tree and I, and my back had bothered me for a spell after that, especially in damp weather; but not for over twenty years.

Snow or no snow, I had time to admire the Kentucky countryside. I'd never seen anything like it. The houses were set well back from the road, leaving room out front for pasture, and most places had horses. The number of horses surprised me. I figured it was a likely state for me to buy the pack horse I wanted, and I would have tried to do so if I'd had thirty or forty dollars.

It was a strange day. We'd seen people and they'd seen us, but no one had stopped us or said a word to us. No one had waved from passing cars, and if it hadn't been for the V signs from truck drivers, I would have suspected the three of us had turned invisible. It didn't mean a thing to Tarzan and Depeche Toi, but it disappointed me, and I felt I'd been hoodwinked since girlhood. Where was all the southern hospitality I'd heard about?

I was thinking this way as we pulled into Lexington about ten that night. We had no place to stay and no money for a hotel, and it was not a night for camping out.

A police car passed us and stopped. "We thought you'd stop along the way in this kind of weather," said the driver. "Follow us."

They led us to a sales stable, and that's were we spent the night. I slept on a cot in the office. The owner said he didn't dare take me to his home. He was a bachelor.

Next morning, he asked how long we'd be staying.

"Until I work off the charges," I said. "I'm pretty handy around horses."

"Now don't talk like that. Southern hospitality starts in stables. What do you think of these other horses? Kentucky raises the finest."

"Grandpa Libby thought that before you were born. He had a mare from down here. Her name was Zara. I rode her bareback many times."

"Probably from the Haggin Farm. They used names like that."

It was around 1900. That's all I could tell him.

While we were talking, some reporters arrived and one of them told me that mail was awaiting me at the post office. I told him that there had to be a mistake. I'd been giving out Springfield, Tennessee as my next mail stop.

"News travels fast," said the reporter. "With the press

coverage you've been getting, every big post office along your route will have mail waiting for you."

He was just guessing, but he proved to be right in the long run. And he was absolutely right that day, for some fifty letters were waiting for me in Lexington. I read a few as we plodded down the highway in the general direction of Tennessee. The first two were from complete strangers in Oregon and New Mexico, and both invited me to make my home with them. Those were the first of many written offers, although I'd already been given the same opportunity by folks I'd stayed with along the road. Those kind people had their hearts in the right place, but none seemed to understand that I didn't want to be dependent on anyone else but me. I valued my independence and I didn't want to lose it. If I ever had a home again, it would have to be an independent home, so to speak. At least, that's the way I felt now. You never know how you're going to feel when you're older.

We made good time once we were out of the city. It was a cloudy day, but warmer than the one before, and my back felt better. Depeche Toi ran around as if he'd never run before, and Tarzan kept to a steady pace. Then when we came to where the road forked, he stopped. I clucked and reined him left, but he just stood there. Left was Tennessee and straight ahead was Louisville, and he was just making sure that I knew where we were going. That horse had a memory.

He was remembering what I'd told him and the dog several times back in New England: A third cousin of mine had moved his family from Augusta to Louisville, Kentucky, just before the second war, and I had a mind to visit them. But now that we were in the same state, Louisville was westward and off our route.

It started to snow. Without any sign from me, Tarzan turned and took the road for Tennessee. He knew where South was.

It snowed for hours. My back started troubling me again.

Every home seemed to have horses, and every road gate was closed. Kentuckians don't let their horses roam, and I didn't blame them. But those closed gates didn't help us. The snow was coming down like cotton, darkness was at hand, and we needed shelter.

It would have been simple to dismount and open a gate, but if we had been turned away, I might not have been able to mount again, feeling the way I did. So I stayed in the saddle and searched for an open gate.

A car stopped alongside us, and a woman rolled down the window and asked, "Going far?"

I told her that I hoped not, but that I hadn't been able to find any gates open along that road.

"Try the third place down on your left," she said. "The gate is usually open. The people have no sense. Their horses are always straying."

She drove on and I counted the places on the left until we came to number three. Sure enough, the gate was open. We turned in, walked up a long drive to the house, and out of the house came the woman who had been in the car. The kind lady had left the gate open for me.

Tarzan went to the barn, and Depeche Toi and I were put up in the house. Lois Ellen Clayton was the woman's name, and their place was a tobacco farm right in the middle of the horse-breeding country. Her husband was away on business, so I never did meet him, but she wasn't alone. She had a little son named Billy, and her grandmother also lived there. The family didn't have any cats, so Depeche Toi played with Billy, and even slept in the boy's room.

The snowstorm lasted another day, but we stayed there a few days longer. Grandma wanted me to see all the glories of Kentucky. I never did find out her exact age, but she was in her nineties and the most talkative person I'd ever met.

"I lie about my age," she'd say, "but I'm not over one hundred. I rode side saddle until I was eighty-seven. I don't know what's going to happen to the country when I'm gone. Young people are so irresponsible these days. Of course, if you're a true sample of Maine, then perhaps there is some hope. I've been reading about you in the papers. You're not like the other youngsters. You have the fine quality of determination, young lady."

She was forever calling me a young lady, and once the roads were clear, she saw to it that I didn't have an idle moment. She had her granddaughter drive me around to see the sights, such as the inside of a big whiskey distillery (all those guards made it look like a prison on the outside), a power plant of the Tennessee Valley Authority, and a big tobacco auction, where I couldn't understand a single thing anyone said.

Little Billy cried when we took to the road again. Depeche Toi had become his pal. The boy felt better when Grandma said, "The young lady needs the brave dog to protect her against Indians." The last thing she said to me was, "Good luck. Come back when you have a free moment, young lady."

Tarzan was well rested and frisky. Now the limp was a thing of the past. But the young lady on top of him wasn't so frisky. My back was feeling better, but I felt tuckered out. I suppose I'd done and seen too much in those few days, but I was ashamed of myself. Grandma could have walked to California on her own two feet.

A crowd was waiting for us in the center of Versailles ("Sailles" as they call it down there). Somebody asked about my folders, and business was brisk for about ten minutes. Then the dog and I lunched on hamburgers provided by a state trooper. When he asked for an autographed folder, I gave it to him but he insisted on paying for it. Then he gave me his autograph. "Save it. May be worth something someday," he said. "I'm writing a book about my experiences."

When we moved off and away from the crowd, the same trooper gave me some advice that may have saved me from arrest at a later date: "Some cities require a license to peddle, so be careful when you sell your folders. Don't offer them for sale. You can still sell them without a license if people ask for them first. So when there's a crowd around, arrange to have somebody ask for a folder and that will start the ball rolling." I thanked him for telling me how to break the law legally.

There was plenty of snow on the ground that day, but no storm. We made good time all afternoon, averaging three miles an hour. Now we were in a section that didn't have fine homes, and many of the places we saw would have been called shacks back in Maine. The people along the way were sharecroppers, and we saw more mules than horses. I wondered if a pack mule wouldn't be cheaper than a horse and work out just as well.

Just at dusk, a little boy came running up to tell me that some people down the road had a barn and wanted us to stay with them. The barn was big and Tarzan shared it with two mules. The house was small and crowded, there being seven children in the family. One of the older girls was a cripple, but the March of Dimes people had helped her, and now she was improved to where she was working and helped to support the others. The girl and the other children had a good education. One of them asked me what college I had attended. "Hardknocks University," I said, but they didn't laugh, and I was sorry that I'd said it. I'd never been as poor as they were, and I'd spent most of my school-age years doing my best to avoid schooling.

We talked about pack mules, and the father told me they worked out ever better than horses. He said he could buy me a traffic-wise one for about fifteen dollars. So I'd have found some relief for Tarzan right then and there, except that we were six dollars short of the fifteen. The folders were helping us get wealthy again, but we still weren't rich enough to buy a mule.

We hadn't advanced more than five miles the next morning when the snow started coming down again. A woman came running out of a gas station and insisted that the road was too dangerous for a horse. "And some fool driver will run over your dog, too!" she added. "You are staying right here!" Her husband was of the same mind.

There was a stable nearby for Tarzan, and the dog and I were given a heated, furnished apartment above the gas station. It was just like having a home of my own again. In fact, I could have made it my home, for I was offered a job in the diner next door. I liked the idea, but I disliked winter more. Somehow, I was going to get away from snow.

Tarzan was frisky the next morning. Too frisky. I had him hitched, but he started dancing when I lifted the saddle to his back. He swung into me and I fell to the frozen ground. From the sudden, sharp pains, I thought both my left arm and shoulder had been broken.

I was taken back to the apartment, and a doctor was called. Fortunately, no bones had been broken. The doctor gave me pills to ease the pain and said that nature and plenty of rest would mend the arm and shoulder. If he found anything wrong, he didn't tell me. But something was wrong, because my left hand wasn't of much use for weeks, and the shoulder pained for a longer time.

We stayed where we were for five days, then took to the road again. I needed help saddling and packing Tarzan that morning and on many another morning, but the help always came without my asking. The people who owned the gas station argued against my going, but I figured that I'd repaid their kindness by becoming a nuisance, and I didn't want to become more of a nuisance.

It was a good day to put extra miles behind us, for both the horse and the dog were well rested, and I was feeling guilty about wasted time. We were still a long way from Tennessee, and I didn't want to spend all of January in Kentucky. So we plodded along until about eight that night before I started looking for a place to stay.

One farmer after another turned us away. It was for our own health, so to speak. Everybody seemed to have distemper. Human distemper, which was something I'd never heard of before. Finally, a man told me, "Go up that dirt road about two miles. You'll find a house and barn. An old couple lives there. I hear they've stayed healthy."

It was sleeting by the time we reached the place, where the "old couple" lived. They turned out to be a brother and sister in their eighties. The sister came to the door and said, "Brother and I were about to start for church, but I'll ask him." I waited there in the sleet not knowing if I could get back on Tarzan again without help, until she came back and told me to take the horse to the barn.

Brother joined me there and helped me unsaddle and unpack Tarzan. We took Depeche Toi to the house with us, where Sister was already setting a table for me. "Brother said he thinks the Lord will understand," she told me, "and that the Lord will forgive us for staying home from church, as we stayed to help you."

They found it hard to believe that I was on my way from Maine to California.

"You have great courage to do so alone," said Sister.

"I'm not alone, really. The horse and the dog are my companions."

"The Lord must be watching over you," decided Brother.

"I'm counting on Him," I admitted. I thought about telling them about the coin tossing, and decided against it. Instead, I told them I'd asked the Lord's approval five times, and He's given it to me four times. "I didn't want to go on asking Him all night," I explained. "It seemed to me that four-out-of-five was approval enough."

"The fifth time He would have been granting Absolution, and He didn't want to go that far," was Brother's reasoning.

"Now let's not get involved, Brother. I'm sure our friend from Maine isn't hiding any sins."

But they must have discussed me that night, for at breakfast Brother started right in asking me about what signs of approval I'd had from the Almighty. I acted as if I didn't hear. I think the truth might have shocked those good Kentuckians. Instead, I told Sister that she was a great biscuit maker.

"Oh, I did hope you would like them. I've heard northerners prefer toast."

"Only city people," I assured her. "The only times I remember having toast as a little girl was when I was ailing." Then I told them about the way Mama made johnny cakes. Two ways, really. The cakes were made with eggs and sugar in the morning, with butter spread on top. For supper, they were made with molasses but no eggs, and we ate them with pork fat or meat gravy.

After breakfast, they helped me saddle and pack Tarzan. Then Brother made steps out of boxes for me, and I had no trouble climbing into the saddle. My left arm and shoulder still pained.

Depeche Toi lingered behind as we rode out of the yard. I had to call him twice before he came. He liked Sister and Brother, but he was a smart dog and knew that I needed his help more than they did.

I'd always thought of Kentucky as flat country, but it wasn't all that way. The main road led us from hills into valleys and up into more hills. Going downhill, I had to hold Tarzan back for fear he'd slip. The grades were steep and there were no rails, not even on curves. The banks on either side of the road fell off sharply, and we could look down on the tops of trees. Once I asked a sheriff why there were no rails, and he explained that the lack of them saved the county money:

"You see, it's cheaper to pick the drunks out of the ravines in the morning rather than put them into jail for the night."

I did a lot of praying every time we went down those steep grades. With no one around to help, they weren't ideal places for me to have another accident. Back at Chadds Ford, and again at the stable, there'd been people around to help, but the only humans I saw on those hills were the drivers of the trucks that were piled high with tobacco barrels. Those barrels were ten times the size of flour barrels, and they swayed when the trucks sped around curves. The dog didn't mind, but Tarzan and I were about equally scared.

On our first night in the hill country, a sheriff put us up in a county jail. He wanted to drive me to a hotel, because staying in the jail meant that I had to sleep in the same cell with a lady prisoner. I didn't mind. She turned out to be a nice person and much better educated than myself. A clean talker who was in for a year.

"I was framed and I don't belong here," she told me, "but I don't mind, because what are twelve months compared to what the Lord will do to the person who framed me? Besides, the food here is real good."

I had to agree. Hot soup, biscuits, bacon and eggs, and rice pudding for supper, and the same for breakfast, except for the pudding. When I told the matron she was a good cook, she said she was from Louisiana where everybody was a good cook. She was kind enough to phone ahead to Glascow and get us an invitation to spend the night with a friend of hers.

And she was also the one who gave me the shortcut directions to Glascow. Four hours later, a school teacher told me that we were further away from the town than when we'd started that morning. I decided then and there that we wouldn't take any more shortcuts. Not without a drawn map, anyway.

The teacher had heard we were coming along the schoolhouse road, and she brought about twenty boys and girls out to meet us. When I told the children that my Grandpa had once owned a Kentucky mare named Zara, one of the boys said the mare was Haggin bred.

"I've heard that before," I said. "Is your name Haggin?"

It wasn't, but that boy and the others sure knew a lot about horses. When they went back to the school house, they were spouting the names of the horses that might have been sire or dam of Zara.

By nightfall, we were on the right road to Glascow but still twenty miles away. We were going through a valley where the homes were spread out, but for an hour I hadn't been able to talk to anyone about shelter. We'd seen children and grownups in a yard, but by the time we got there they would have disappeared. I'd shout, but no one would answer, so we'd go on to the next place. It seemed peculiar.

Then a car came along and stopped. The driver, a young man, said, "You're out late. How far are you going?"

"The shortest possible distance. I can't seem to find a place to stay."

"Why, there are lots of places," he said, and then he started laughing. "I'll explain later. You're coming home with me. The house up on the hill there. I'll go ahead and wait for you."

He lived with his parents, and they had a television set; that's how he knew who I was. The other people along the road didn't have television, and they thought that I was a man on horseback, and that meant gypsy to them. I'd come along at just the wrong time, right in the middle of a gypsy scare. According to the young man, the gypsies were stealing everything in sight, and the people wanted no part of any stranger.

The young man offered to show me a shortcut to Glascow the next morning, but I told him that we liked the main road.

It snowed again that day, and we didn't reach Glasgow until late at night. A man directed us to the home of the matron's friend, but the friend wasn't there. It was understandable. We were a full day late.

Nearby was a house with a barn. One light was on in the house. I rode into the yard and started shouting, and finally a man opened the door and asked what I wanted.

"I'm looking for a place to stay."

"You ought to be arrested, disturbing people in the middle of the night. I'm not taking care of any bums! Now get going, or I'll call the police!"

"I'm not moving," I said, hoping that he would call the police. Depeche Toi started barking at the man. He went back into the house and slammed the door behind him.

We didn't budge. Some of the neighbors came out of their houses and walked over to us. They knew who we were, and I sold a few folders. Then the man who had called me a bum came out of his house.

"I'm sorry I didn't recognize you," he said. "The police are coming for you. They told me to take care of your horse." Now he was friendly.

"I'll pay for the horse," I said.

"You will not! Now don't treat me like a bum, just because I thought you were one."

So Tarzan spent the night in the man's barn, and Depeche Toi and I were guests of the police in the Glascow jail. Some of the most comfortable beds in America are found in Kentucky jails. We fared well there and all through the rest of the state.

A rainy week in Scottsville, where we were guests of the Jacksonian Hotel. Andrew Jackson stayed there once, and his room was kept just as he'd left it. He probably stayed for more than a week. The hotel didn't charge us a penny; nor did the beauty parlor that gave me my first permanent wave, and made me look ten years younger; nor did the shoe store that gave me a rugged pair of shoes with rubber composition soles that would be just right after we outdistanced winter. I sold a few folders every day and talked on several radio programs. I was interviewed by the press too. They took good care of us in Scottsville, and the hotel wanted us to stay longer. But I was coughing again and my back was acting up. It didn't seem right to repay the town by turning into an invalid.

Then there was Franklin, where the first house with a

barn was owned by the Mayor. So we became the guests of the Mayor and his wife. He was also the head doctor at the hospital there, and the next day I became the guest of the hospital. Several doctors examined me and took tests. Among other things, they found a local infection and gave me sulfa pills to cure it. "Otherwise," the Mayor told me, "all that you need is a good, long rest."

"I plan on doing that as soon as I get to Springfield, Tennessee."

He shook his head and said, "You won't have a chance. I hear the whole city is waiting for you."

When we crossed the border into Tennessee that day, I turned Tarzan around, called Depeche Toi close, and said to them, "Take a last look at Kentucky. It's been good to us."

And it had been good to us. But I didn't feel sad about leaving it, for at long last we were leaving winter behind. I was sure of it! Now we were in a genuine southern state. It had taken over four months to get here, but at last we were through with snow.

The first sizeable town in Tennessee wasn't waiting for us, only a man and his wife were, and they came rushing out of a restaurant as we came to the front of the place. It was the biggest restaurant I'd ever seen, and they owned it.

Until that night, I'd never even seen a piece of pizza, but by the time supper was over I guess I'd sampled every sort of pizza ever invented. The waiters kept raving about the special sauce on the spaghetti, but I didn't touch that dish. I wanted to, but there was no room left in me.

There were hundreds of people dining there, and all were well dressed. In my tramp clothes, I felt as out of place as I had back in that fancy hotel in Springfield, Massachusetts. The others looked at me and smiled while I ate, and afterwards they crowded around my table asking questions and buying folders. I sat there until midnight, talking and autographing. Some individuals wanted as many as twenty folders.

It was the biggest business I'd done on the road. I sold out!

My "pony," as the restaurant owner called Tarzan, rested in the garage while Depeche Toi and I stayed with the family in their living quarters, which were right next to the kitchen. That room was full of big, special stoves for making pizzas, and we had breakfast there the next morning. It was a surprise breakfast in honor of me, I was told. "A Maine Breakfast" they called it: Italian bread, fried lobster tails, hot clam broth with little shrimps in it; and red wine for them. It was a surprise all right. I don't imagine those good people had ever been to Maine.

Then my friends and I set off for Springfield. It was a bright clear day in March, and we made steady time until about noon. It felt good to be in Tennessee and away from winter at last, but the feeling changed when the sky darkened and the snow started coming down. A strong north wind helped push us along through a sudden storm that had all the earmarks of a real Maine blizzard. I started looking for a house with a barn and finally found one. Unlike Kentucky, barns were as scarce as hen's teeth in that part of Tennessee.

Robert E. Lee and his wife welcomed us and made us feel right at home, but they didn't tell me until morning that they had a sick child. They had three cats, so Depeche Toi was happy, and there were horses in the barn, so Tarzan was happy, too.

"You were wise to stop," said Mr. Lee, who was not related to the famous general of the same name. "The radio says this is a big storm. Very unusual weather for this time of year, I can tell you."

The Lee home was south of Orlinda and ten miles from Springfield. Something was wrong with the heating system and the house was colder than the barn. I would have been happy to stay right there and wait out the storm, but I was coughing again and Mrs. Lee felt I'd be safer in a warm place. When the radio said the storm would last for several days, the Lees arranged things so that the sheriff would pick me up and drive me to a Springfield hotel. They said I could

91

leave my friends with them until I was ready to travel again.

The sheriff arrived in the late afternoon. "I'm taking you to the best hotel in Springfield," he said, "and you might as well plan on a long stay. When this storm passes, the roads will be too icy for a horse. This is very unusual weather for Tennessee."

"Is this an expensive hotel?"

"Very, but don't let it worry you. The hotel won't charge you for anything. If you don't mind, we'll stop at my place first. My wife wants to meet you."

His wife also wanted to feed me, so I had supper with her while the sheriff went on about his duties. When he came back for me, she said, "I wish we had a room where you could stay, so I could talk more with you."

Their place was a small one adjoining the jail. I asked if the jail was full.

"No, but you don't want to stay there," said the sheriff.

"If it's warm and dry, it's as good a place to stay as any. How about it?"

"But the windows are barred!" his wife objected. "You can't sleep behind bars."

"Yes, I can," I insisted. "I've enjoyed many a night of sound sleep behind bars in recent weeks."

So I never did get to see the inside of that expensive hotel in Springfield. Instead, I settled down in the jail's cell for women. It occupied a whole floor and had twenty-eight beds, and I was the only person in residence.

"I hope you're different from the last woman we had in here," said the sheriff. "She was from Texas, and she came close to wrecking the place. Smashed windows, beds, chairs and the bathtub. Cost plenty to repair. If you were from Texas, I don't think I'd let you stay here."

I promised not to smash any windows, and I stayed there for ten days. One of the newspapers reported that I was holding court in the city jail, and that wasn't far from wrong, for everybody from the Mayor to groups of school children came to visit me. Meeting the children was the most fun. The teachers lined them up, I'd shake hands with every one of them, and then they started asking questions. For the most part, they wanted to know what I'd seen and done on my trip. The girls were more interested in Tarzan than the dog. The teachers wanted to know about politics in Maine. "Regular as a clock," I told them.

So I didn't lack for company, and I stayed in jail most of the time. It was cold outside, and on one of my few trips into that cold I arranged to have some postcards printed with me and my friends on the front. Folders would have been too expensive. As it was, the one thousand postcards ran eight-and-a-half-cents apiece (the cut alone cost twenty-five dollars), which didn't allow much profit when sold for a dime, although people usually gave me more than that. I can remember when the post office sold penny cards. I don't know how the government did it.

My cough improved to the point of almost disappearing while I stayed in jail. I really had a rest, although I had to talk too much and my voice got hoarse. Still, the left arm was useable again, the shoulder was only a touch sore, and I figured I was in the best shape since leaving home. Regular eating helped, of course. I had lunch and supper every day with the sheriff and his wife, but took breakfast in jail so as not to be a bother. Breakfast was hardy, because most of the jail's inmates worked on the road chain-gang. It was always the same: Cereal, cuddle potatoes with green onions mixed in (a favorite of Uncle Waldo), hot biscuits, sorghum, blackeyed peas and extra good coffee.

I had plenty of reading matter in that jail, and all of it was in the form of correspondence. My mail caught up with me, and it amounted to more than five hundred letters and cards from people who were complete strangers. Many of them invited me to stay with them when I reached their part of the country; a few wanted me to make my permanent home with them. The only invitation I felt I should accept was the one from Mrs. Casey Jones of Jackson, Tennessee. She was the widow of the famous railroad engineer who saved the passengers and died himself. He was a real hero. Uncle Waldo knew two poems by heart. One was about Casey Jones, the railroad engineer, and the other was about a Casey who was a baseball player. I suppose I'd heard him recite each poem about ten thousand times, but I never tired of hearing the Casey Jones one. So I wrote his widow and said I would be along shortly.

The snow and ice were about gone when I got back to the Lee place near Orlinda. Tarzan and Depeche Toi had been in such good hands that they didn't want to leave. It was the first time I had to lead Tarzan from any place. He kept throwing back his head and stopping as we went down the road to Springfield. I didn't dare mount him until we were out of sight of the Lee home, and long after that I had to keep a sharp eye on the dog and call to him. My friends had enjoyed themselves too much. I kept telling them that California was just around the corner and that it was warm out there, but they didn't give a hoot.

The three of us were rested and in prime shape for travel, and I was confident that we'd make a good twenty miles a day on those fine, hard Tennessee roads. We were headed for Jackson and the promised visit with Mrs. Casey Jones. The route wasn't on a direct line with California, but somehow it seemed important for me to meet the wife of a famous person. I would have gone there even if I'd known the five-day trip would take much longer than that.

We didn't make good time for all sorts of reasons. First, there was the traffic. Every car and truck in the state seemed to be on the roads, and there were times when they came so thick and fast that we just had to step aside and wait on the shoulders. It was a safety measure, but stepping off the road meant stepping into soft, muddy clay. Tarzan would sink in over his hoofs and slip sideways. A horse with no load could have stepped along without trouble, but Tarzan was carrying plenty. Then it started to rain. It seemed as if the state had been saving all of its unusual weather for us.

So we'd cover ten miles one day and five the next. We

94

spent the nights along the way in stables, and when there wasn't room for me, the sheriff of the jail where I'd slept the night before would come and get me and drive me back to the same jail.

It was slow going, but we worked our way through Ashland and over a river and up into mountain country. There the roads seemed poorer and the mud was certainly deeper. The higher we climbed, the harder it rained. When a stable owner told me that it wouldn't rain forever, but that it would rain for the next few days, I decided to unload and stay right there until the sun broke through again.

They wouldn't let me camp in the stable, so I left the horse and dog there and became the guest of the local jail, which was three miles away. The sheriff invited me to stay as long as I wanted. I slept on top of four mattresses in a storeroom. During the day, I sat most of the time in his office, writing in my diary and answering letters.

That little town was somewhere north of Dickson, and it was full of horse lovers. Several of them got in the habit of dropping by to talk to me. Most of their talk was about Tennessee Walkers, and most of mine was about Tarzan. I don't know when those men went home or attended to business. When they weren't visiting me they were up at the stable with Tarzan.

On my third day there, one of my new acquaintances, a Mr. Richards, invited me to his house for lunch. Of them all, his was the only name I learned, and I still wouldn't know it if he hadn't introduced Mrs. Richards to me. It was a fine lunch, and afterwards they said they wanted to show me the most beautiful sight in Tennessee. I didn't think we'd see much of a view in the rain, but they insisted, so we drove about five miles to a farm.

"Over there," said Mr. Richards, pointing to a big, weathered barn that had needed paint for a good many years.

"It is beautiful," I agreed. I felt I should be polite.

"Just wait until you see the inside," Mrs. Richards said. We walked across the yard and entered the barn. About twenty men and women were waiting for us. They smiled, but the only one who said anything was Mr. Richards: "All right, Harry, bring him out." Then he turned to me and said, "We read in the papers that you needed a second horse and couldn't find a good one at the right price. Now let's find out what you think of this one."

The horse's name was Rex. He was a big, solid bay and stood about two hands taller than Tarzan. I liked his looks, even if he did have four white feet. "A horse with four white feet is only good for the crows," is an old Maine saying, but I'd known some fine horses that were marked that way.

"He's a Tennessee Walking Horse," Mr. Richards explained.

I knew that from looking at him, but I nodded my thanks for the information. I looked at Rex's teeth and judged him to be over fifteen. "How old?" I asked.

"Twenty. He's always been a pet horse and he's used to traffic."

I stood there studying Rex, and I liked everything I saw. Even his tail was natural. It hadn't been broken and set up where it didn't belong, which they always do for show purposes. The only thing that troubled me about him was his size. "How would a shorty like me climb on top of such a giant?" I asked.

I found out right quick. "Stretch!" Harry said to Rex. The horse moved his hind legs back and his fore legs forward. That brought his back down until it was lower than Tarzan's.

They saddled him, and I rode him around inside the barn for a few minutes. He had a nice, easy-going gait. The breed was developed for comfortable riding, and Rex didn't disgrace the breed. Sitting on him was like sitting in an easy chair. In comparison, Tarzan was a rocking boat.

I stopped him and said "Stretch!" Down went his back, and I dismounted. "I won't ask about the price," I said. "I like him, but I just can't afford him."

96

"The price is right," Mr. Richards said, "and we think you can afford him. As a matter of fact, we've already seen to the cost. Just tell people along the way that Rex comes from Tennessee."

They trucked Rex over to the stable for me, and there he met Tarzan and Depeche Toi. My friends seemed to sense that the newcomer belonged to the family, and they didn't give him any trouble. Tarzan was smart enough to know that Rex would make the journey easier, and Depeche Toi liked horses almost as much as cats.

A friend of Mr. Richards gave me an old saddle. The rain stopped—the sun came out. It was a great day there in the mountains of Tennessee.

Now we were four: Tarzan, Depeche Toi, Rex and myself. For the first few days, Rex wasn't much help. He was soft, for he'd not been ridden in months, so I didn't ride him much; Tarzan carried me most of the time and the cargo all of the time. Even so, Rex was wet with sweat at the end of each day on the road. And with those long legs of his, his gait was faster than Tarzan's. Five miles an hour was nothing to him, whereas Tarzan had to press to do better than three. So if I didn't hold Rex back, Tarzan had to jog, and he was carrying the load.

Then it started raining again, and by the end of that day, Rex was coughing. We were in Dickson, then, and I pulled into the first stable we saw. The owner's wife invited me to stay at her house.

By morning, Rex had developed a bad cold and his coughing was worse. I was told not to worry and that he'd be all right, but I wasn't about to take him on the road again in this condition. As it was, his cold got worse before it took a turn for the better, and we stayed over in Dickson for five days. I spent most of those days hunting for a saddle. The gift one wasn't right for either horse.

Thanks to the stable owner, I finally located a nearly new

officer's saddle with wooden stirrups and skirts that was a perfect fit for Rex. I got it at a bargain price, and buying it cost me half my ready cash. But it was a necessity, not a luxury. The man who sold it to me said that he was losing money on the deal. "Considering what you've set out to do at your age, I'd be losing more if you were a man, because I'd give it to you," he told me. "I learned long ago that when you give a woman anything, all you get in return is trouble, and I've had enough trouble in my life."

Tarzan, Depeche Toi and I got weighed in Dickson. The horse had gained eighty-six pounds since leaving Maine. Depeche Toi had dropped two pounds, but he looked in better shape than ever. And I had gained seven pounds! The figures didn't prove anything, except that you can lose weight running, but not walking or sitting.

But other figures proved that Tarzan was a remarkably strong horse. With me in the saddle and the cargo on his back, he'd been carrying a maximum load for a twelve hundred pound pack horse, and he weighed less than ten hundred. So Tarzan had been overloaded right along! Right then and there I decided not to baby Rex any longer. As soon as he was fit, he'd have to start sharing the load.

So he was carrying me and a hundred pounds of our possessions when we set out from Dickson for the Tennessee River and Camden and on down to Jackson. Every day, I added a bit more weight to Rex's back, and he learned to pace himself so that Tarzan didn't have to jog to stay close.

No matter which horse I was on, both of them wanted to get their noses out front. They'd move along side by side, but sometimes the lead horse wouldn't be in the lead. Their system worked fine, except in times of heavy traffic. Then the four of us would have to move off the road and into the mud. In that season of the year, Tennessee must be the muddiest state in the country.

It was the mud that gave me the idea for Depeche Toi to ride. I'd tried him once or twice on Tarzan by holding him on the saddle, but he hadn't enjoyed the bouncing. But there was no bounce in Rex's back, and the dog didn't mind riding on him for short spells. I fixed the blanket rolls so they were sort of flat over Rex's flanks, and that made a fine seat or bed for Depeche Toi, depending upon how tired he was. He'd bark when he wanted to ride, because he had to be lifted on, but he'd jump off without help when he was tired of riding.

I was careful not to overwork Rex, and he was shaping into hard condition by the time we reached Jackson and the home of Mrs. Casey Jones. But we'd run into another rainy spell, and the dampness hadn't helped him. He was coughing again and his nose was running.

Mrs. Jones owned a small stable. She took one look at Rex and phoned the vet. He came right over, but he didn't think there was anything seriously wrong with the horse.

"He doesn't want to eat," I said. "Just picks at his food."

"Well, he doesn't have a fever. Maybe you've been pushing him too much. He's still soft. He'll shake this with a couple of days' rest, and his appetite will pick up on the road."

I'd planned on just an overnight visit in Jackson, but I was there four days before Rex looked ready for travel. By that time, Mrs. Jones and I were about talked out. I'd heard all about her husband and she'd heard all about Uncle Waldo, and we also educated each other about Maine and Tennessee. The papers and the radio brought many people to the stable, and business with the postcards was steady.

Rex seemed fine on the fifth morning. It was a warm, clear day when he headed down the road for Memphis. I figured we'd make that city in four days, and we did. Along the way, I learned two things about my new horse: He didn't like bridges, and he couldn't swim as well as Tarzan (we had to ford two rivers) .

All four of us walked into Memphis, and both horses were limping. Rex's shoes hadn't been meant for hard roads, and he needed new ones all around. Tarzan hadn't been shod since Philadelphia, and his rears had worn and broken.

A police car came alongside us and stopped. "Where have you been?" asked the driver. "We expected you hours ago."

"I've been on the way, but I've been walking. Both horses need shoes."

"We have a stable ready for you. The shortest route is down this parkway. It's one way, but it will be all right for you to go against the traffic. Stay on the side, go through the underpass, and we'll meet you at the other end. We want to get you there before darkness."

There weren't many cars on the parkway, and we walked along against the light traffic for about two miles without any trouble. Then two cars stopped and about ten young fellows piled out of them.

"Where do you think you're going?" one asked.

"I'm heading for a stable," I said.

"Oh, you're a woman? A woman bum! This is a one-way parkway and you're going the wrong way."

"I know it," I explained, "but the police told me to come this way. It's the shortest route to the stable, and they want me off the streets before dark."

All ten argued with me and insisted that we turn around and go back to the far end of the parkway. They didn't care if it took us all night to get to the stable, and they cared less about the condition of my horses.

Finally, the smallest young fellow there yelled, "What are we waiting for? If she won't do it, we will! Grab the horses! Let's show this crazy old woman how things are done in Memphis!"

He pushed me and tore the lead ropes from my hands. With that, Depeche Toi dove for him and grabbed him by a trouser leg. The dog knew something was wrong, but the horses just stood there, more or less unconcerned. The other fellows laughed and shouted, and two of them kicked at the dog. Then somebody grabbed my arms and told the others to take the horses.

I heard the brakes of a car. It was the same police car.

100

They had figured something was wrong and had come looking for me.

"What's going on here?" asked the driver.

"Nothing much," said one of the fellows. "We were just talking to this sweet old lady."

"You're just old enough to find out how expensive talking can be," the other policeman said. "Who owns these cars? It's illegal to stop on this parkway."

It was dark by the time the policemen were through checking licenses and papers and names. As I stood there watching, I was thinking that it was only the second time on my journey that people had tried to trouble me, and each time the people had been young, but old enough to know better. I didn't try to understand them. At times, I didn't understand myself.

One of the policemen walked with us to the stable, just to make sure there'd be no more trouble. He said I could press charges against the young fellows for attempting to steal my horses, but I didn't. I wasn't hunting trouble for myself or anyone else.

It was a first class, quality stable. I could tell that from the looks of the place and the fine animals in the stalls, and from the way the men handled my horses. It wasn't the sort of stable where I could stay, but the men were very helpful and promised to have a blacksmith there first thing in the morning. It was all right for Depeche Toi to remain there and guard the rigging. I hadn't taught him to do that, he'd made it his business along the way to turn himself into a watchdog, and people knew what he meant when he growled.

Everyone there, including the police, thought that I had a place to stay, but I didn't. So after my boys were fed and watered, I walked out into the night and started looking for a cheap hotel. Without my boys, nobody recognized me. It was the same as New Year's Eve back in Philadelphia. Everybody thought that I was a bum, and nobody was interested in telling me where a hotel was.

Finally, a man who was on the tipsy side pointed out a Salvation Army building to me. "The men's quarters are full," the Army man told me. When I showed him my post-card, he apologized. Supper, a bed, a nightgown and break-fast cost me one dollar. The Army man didn't want to take my money, but I insisted. For some reason, they couldn't let me stay there another night, but they did direct me to a rooming house run by an Irishman. I reserved a room there before going back to the stable.

The sun was out that morning, but the day was bitter cold. April in Memphis was colder than any April I could remember in Maine. "Unusual weather we're having," they told me at the stable. I wondered if the state ever had usual weather.

Tarzan was shod that day, but the blacksmith wanted to wait forty-eight hours before fixing Rex. "This Walker's feet are already sore," he told me. "Been used to hard ground and not pavements for most of his life, I'd say."

When I asked about charges, he said they wouldn't run to much. The labor would be free, he explained, and he would give me the shoes at cost. That sounded reasonable enough until I found out what shoes cost in Memphis. I had barely enough to pay for them, and just pennies to support myself for the next few days.

Well, I settled that little problem by wandering around the city with Tarzan and Depeche Toi. We sold close to eight dollars worth of postcards in six hours. That was enough for two nights in the rooming house and meals. I came close to freezing to death on the first night, and didn't dare take my outdoor garments off. The landlord gave me a little oil stove the second night, but it wasn't much help. Indoors and outdoors in Memphis, I was thankful for my union suit.

We were seventeen cents away from being dead broke when we left Memphis and headed for the bridge over the Mississippi. For once, I was happy to be delayed by groups of people along the way. I sold at least three postcards every time.

There was a wide steel expansion plate at the beginning of the bridge. I was on Rex, and he wanted no part of that plate. He backed away from it, snorting, and turned around and around. We attracted a good audience and heard plenty of advice, but none of it worked. Finally, a man tried to lead Rex across the plate. The Walking Horse just didn't want to walk on that metal. He pulled back, lost his balance and slammed into Tarzan's shoulder.

That irritated Tarzan. He laid his ears back, took a pinch of Rex's neck in his teeth, and yanked hard. Rex went across that plate without really knowing what he was doing.

He minded his manners crossing the rest of the bridge, but I had my hands full as soon as the Mississippi River was at our backs. The big bay kept trying to turn on me, as if he wanted to go back over the river. He acted as if he knew we were in Arkansas, and he was already homesick for Tennessee.

7 🐖 ARKANSAS—MISSOURI

I'd never been there, but I was not a complete stranger to Arkansas. My Papa used to take off from Maine now and then to seek his fortune elsewhere, and back in 1922 he'd tried his luck in Arkansas. "You just like to travel," Mama had told him when he'd come back home without a fortune, which was always the case. But we heard all about the state from him, so the trip hadn't been a total loss.

There I was—in the April of my sixty-third year—the second member of my family ever to set foot in Arkansas. And just like my father, I was walking down the road from the Mississippi to Forrest City. Of course, I was sitting and the horses were doing the walking, whereas my father had walked the same sixty miles on his own two feet. And the 1922 road was now a highway.

Papa had gone to Forrest City to look for a big paying job. I was there just to pass through it and get a little closer to California.

It was a long, lonely highway through flat country where they raised peaches and cotton. Traffic was light most of the time, but when it came it was usually in spells and we didn't waste time getting far to the side. I was told that the most reckless driving in the world takes place on that highway, and from what I saw, I believed it. They were the fastest drivers in the world, too. I called it "Horror Road," because of all the dead dogs and wild things I saw. Depeche Toi didn't like it one bit, but I kept him on a rope and made sure he stayed close.

The towns seemed to be arranged for our convenience. We always managed to reach one along about dusk. A crowd would gather, and I'd sell some postcards. Why, they treated me as if I was a movie star. Uncle Waldo would have thought that I was at least as important as Tom Mix. And every time, somebody offered to shelter me and my friends for the night. Some very nice people lived in the towns along Horror Road.

The lady who took Depeche Toi and me to her home the first night also arranged for a retired doctor to put up Tarzan and Rex in his barn. The man didn't look old enough to be a doctor, but it was a fact that he had been one but now he was retired.

"You look too young to be retired," I told him.

"That's just why I retired," he explained. "I look so young that nobody has faith in me. What are you taking for that cough?"

"It's nothing. Just dust from the road."

"You see? You don't think I know anything, either."

He wouldn't say a word to me after that, but I noticed that he gave the horses some darned good hay, sweet as new mown. Tarzan was holding up a hog's mouthful as I left, and Rex was stuffing himself faster than I'd seen him do it before.

Next morning, the retired doctor apologized for not having any grain on hand. "When you're on the move, your horses should have grain every day," he advised.

I nodded and said, "I know. I carried it at first, but I wanted to cut down on Tarzan's load. Now that I have two horses, I'll start doing it again. Is there a feed store in town?"

He told me where it was and added, "People take my advice about animals. I should have been a veterinarian."

He laughed when he said it. Otherwise, I might have recited the poem that had been in my folder—the one that started with, "If you think you're beaten, you are. . . ." I rode Tarzan when we went to the feed store that morning, and all the way I wished that I had told the poem. It might have done the young doctor some good. Just twelve months before, I sure thought I had been beaten. I'd believed that I was going back to the farm to die, and had been too dumb to realize that the contract to grow pickles was really His grant for me to carry on awhile longer. Now I was beginning to wonder if all things are foreordained.

I bought a hundred pounds of corn and told the feed man to tie the sack in the middle and use two strings to tie the open end. That way, the weight was even across Rex's back. Well, the feed man knew better. One string on the end was enough, he assured me. I didn't argue, because he did everything else right, and also tied the sack secure to the back of Rex's saddle.

We hadn't gone a hundred yards from the feed store toward Horror Road when the end string gave way and fifty pounds of corn kernels poured to the ground. Right in the middle of town! A policeman helped me scoop up the corn, and a little boy hurried to the feed store to tell the man what had happened. The feed man came on the run and brought more string with him so that he could retie the sack.

"I know you said to use two pieces of string, but one should have held," he mentioned. "The trouble was that I used poor quality string."

Now he used three pieces of string to tie the sack's end. I didn't say anything, but it looked like the same poor quality string to me. And I was darn mad at first, but then I reminded myself that all things are foreordained.

"All right, boys," I said to my horses. "Clean it up." I took their bridles off, and Tarzan and Rex lowered their heads and went after the corn that was still on the ground.

106

It was scattered all over the road, and they cleaned it up as if they'd not eaten in weeks. I had to hold Depeche Toi, or he would have helped. He was one of my "boys," of course, but dogs can't digest raw corn. On the other hand, many a dog has thrived on fried corn meal.

In Maine, spilled milk or spilled anything else means bad luck. In Arkansas, spilled corn means good luck, as I learned that morning. I'd rebridled the horses and climbed aboard Tarzan again when a reporter arrived and told me that a motel fifteen miles to the west had invited us to spend the night there.

I didn't know if it would be smart to stop there or not. It was a nice day and I wanted to make more mileage than that, but when we reached the motel I noticed it had a stable. Cars had to park outdoors, but not horses. Uncle Waldo would have approved.

So we pulled in there and received royal treatment. It was one of the biggest motels I'd seen, and the first one where I stayed. The manager bought a stack of my cards, and I sold about fifty more to other guests during supper hour in the long dining room. When I told the manager's wife how nice smelling the bath soap was, she gave me a supply for future use. So all in all it turned out to be a lucky day for me, and I noted in my diary that it might be a good idea to spill a little corn on the road every morning.

We were four more days on the road before reaching Forrest City. We found stables where they allowed me to sleep the first two nights. I was looking for another stable toward dusk the next day when an elderly man stopped his car and invited us to stay over at his place. He said his wife would be happy to have us, and gave me the directions to get there. Then he drove ahead and waited for me in his yard. When we pulled in, he said, "Take the horses down to the barn. I'll be down in a few minutes and help you unload."

I had all the gear off by the time he arrived. "You should

have waited," he said. "Now sit down and let me take over with the feed and water. I told my wife that you're here and she's delighted. She's readying supper now."

We were still in the barn when a bell sounded from the house. "That means supper is ready," explained the man. "Make yourself comfortable. I'll bring it to you."

Then he left me in the barn while he went into the house. I had expected to eat in the house and sleep there, too, but I ended up doing both things in the barn. I was provided with a cot and blankets, so I wasn't at all uncomfortable, but it did seem odd that I wasn't invited to the house to meet his wife, at least. I figured they had a fight about my being there.

But the mystery cleared up when the man brought my breakfast in the morning. He explained that his wife hadn't been out of their house in several years and had some fear of meeting people. She wouldn't even see old friends. "I was sure she'd want to meet you, because she's been reading about you in the papers and talking about you," he explained. "But I was wrong. I guess she'll be this way for the rest of her life. Except for this fear of people, she's fine. Doctor's can't help. She won't talk to doctors, either."

He helped me saddle and pack the horses that morning. I was just about to thank him and say goodbye when the bell rang up at the house, and he hurried off. I mounted Rex, and as my boys and I walked toward the road, the man came out of the house and called to me. Then his wife came out of the house. She was carrying a paper bag.

She was a tiny woman with a pretty face and a shy smile. Her hair was jet black, and she looked to be twenty or thirty years younger than her husband. She came right up to where I was waiting on Rex and handed me the paper bag. Didn't say a thing, just kept smiling and nodding. Then she bent down and patted Depeche Toi on the head. He licked her hand.

"My wife prepared some lunch for you," the man explained.

108

"Thank you," I said to her, "You are very kind."

She looked up at me. Her lips moved, but she didn't say anything. Then she turned and ran back into the house.

"At least she came out of the house," her husband said. "First time in years. Maybe she's improving."

I gave him one of my postcards and asked him to give it to his wife. On it, I wrote: "Thank you again for being so kind to an old, lady tramp."

I felt so sorry for that woman. From what I saw of her, I'd say she hadn't led a hard life, yet something had gone wrong. But she wasn't an unright person. If she had been, Depeche Toi wouldn't have licked her hand.

It took us six hours to cover the last eight miles into Forrest City. More and more people were stopping us, and I was down to my last dozen postcards when we reached the city's outskirts. I stopped by a little printing plant to order a new supply. Since I'd already had the cut, the cost was cheaper than the time before, and I was able to pay for two thousand cards.

I had to wait a day before I could pick up the cards. Then a reporter who interviewed me asked to borrow the cut. He promised to mail it on to me, but he never did. So although I didn't know it at the time, my first day in Forrest City cost me twenty-five dollars, and I wasn't a wealthy woman. Of course, that was an old cut and it didn't show Rex, so perhaps it happened for the best.

The wait stretched into four days. Two television stations wanted me for some of their shows, and one of the television ladies put up the dog and me at her apartment. Depeche Toi was the real star of the shows. When we were on camera, he spent most of the time sitting on a table with his paws up, or leaning over and kissing me. He did the same thing on two radio shows, and I didn't have the heart to tell him that none of his acting was being seen. Back in Maine, he'd been just an ordinary dog and knew it. But by now he must have sensed that he was something special and was starting to act important. How many dogs walk from coast to coast?

There was quite a dent in my new supply of postcards by the time we left Forrest City. Thanks to television, radio and the press, everybody seemed to recognize me, whether my boys were with me or not.

So it was one stop after the other on the morning we worked our way west of the city. The cards continued to sell like hot cakes. On one of those stops I met the man who was riding his bicycle all over the country and getting signatures from the governors of the states. He'd already been into Maine, and he had only four states to go. "When I get off this bike," he told me, "I'll never get on another one of the darn things. The money is good, but I wouldn't do it again for ten times as much. You'll feel the same way, if you reach California. You won't want to look at a horse ever again."

"You're wrong," I told him. "Horses are friendly. I don't know about bicycles. Never owned one."

He asked for my card and had me autograph it for him, and then he autographed a personal card of his and gave it to me—and on it he had written: "To the cleverest woman, young or old, I've ever met."

"Why am I so clever?" I asked.

"Because you've managed to keep the secret so long. Now we know who is paying you to make this trip. I thought right along that it was a publicity stunt. It's a great gag."

Then he told me that it was all in the morning papers. Out in Cheyenne, Wyoming, they hold a big rodeo shindig as a tourist attraction every July, and they'd invited me to join the parade on the opening day. I was one of the last persons in America to hear about the invitation, and I heard it from the bicycle man who thought I was being paid to help promote the rodeo. "If you know anybody out there," I told my informer, "tell them that the rest of Arkansas and then Missouri, Kansas and Colorado stand between me and Wyoming. The month of May begins tomorrow, and I don't

110

know where I'll be in July. And if you can collect what you think they're paying me, I'll split it with you."

He wasn't the only one who thought that the rodeo people were paying me. Depeche Toi and I checked in at a motel because I didn't like the looks of the sky. The houses were scarce along that stretch of highway. The first thing the motel manager said was, "I hope those Wyoming people are paying you a lot of money. I think it's terrible of them to use a woman your age for a publicity stunt."

"If they're paying me, I wish they'd tell me about it," I said.

He didn't know whether to believe me or not, and he said as much. "I half believe you, and I half don't, so I'll charge you half rate." And that's what he did.

Rex and Tarzan stayed in a neighbor's corral with seven mares and a stallion, but they didn't stay long. About midnight, the heavens opened up and the rain came down by the buckets. It pounded down hour after hour so that I couldn't sleep, and it made so much noise on the roof that for some minutes I didn't hear the motel manager pounding on the door. He'd received a phone call about three in the morning from the neighbor who owned the corral. The neighbor had just checked on the horses and found some rails down and all the inmates gone except the stallion. He had been unable to find the horses anywhere and had already notified the police.

"There's nothing you can do in this rain," the motel man said. "I'll keep you posted if there's any news. Go back to sleep."

I got dressed instead and went over to the motel office and sat there until breakfast time, and then I didn't have any appetite for anything more than black coffee. I felt lower than I had on any day since leaving Maine. There I was, somewhere in Arkansas, with California still a long way off and no horses to get me there. Depeche Toi seemed to sense what a pickle we were in. He was so gloomy that he just curled up in a corner and didn't even attempt to give my hand comforting licks when I patted him.

The motel man was talkative, but he didn't say much to lift my spirits. "Looks like a two-day rain. If they stay off the road, nobody will spot them," he'd say, or, "If they get as far as the cypress swamps, it may be weeks before they're found," or, "Those cottonmouth in the swamps have killed many a horse and cow." I'd heard about those snakes and the swamps from my Papa, and remembering what he'd said in the long ago didn't cheer me any, either.

It was late afternoon when the police called to report that a motorist had spotted a herd of horses going single file down a road. A black horse (Tarzan) was in the lead, and seven mares were strung out behind him, and then came a big bay (Rex). The herd was traveling in the direction of a village about ten miles from where I sat.

Three hours later, the police called again and said that the mares had been caught but that the black horse and the bay had dodged them and run off. It was dark and still raining hard by then, and the police didn't intend to look any more that night.

"You haven't had a bite to eat all day and you can't live on coffee," said the motel man. "Now have something to eat and get a good night's sleep. I sure hope your horses don't find the swamps."

I had more coffee, forced myself to eat a piece of pie, and then went back to my room to get some sleep. I could hardly keep my eyes open, but sleep was a long time coming. Worry kept me awake, and so did that rain pounding on the roof. And once in awhile I'd think I heard the motel man knocking on the door, but that was always in my imagination. I'd open the door each time anyway, hoping for good news, then I'd climb back into bed.

Finally, I did something that I didn't want to do, but doing it somehow helped me get to sleep: I prayed an asking prayer. My Papa had taught me to never ask direct help from the Lord. "If you're deserving, you don't need to ask, for

112

He will help you. If you're undeserving, then He has every right not to help, and you're wasting His time and yours."

But that night I just had to break Papa's golden rule. I had my health, my dog, my gear and eighteen dollars or so, but I still needed help to get to California. "I hate to bother You," I prayed, "and I thank Thee for permission to go to California, but I didn't plan on walking there and the dog is a touch small for carrying the gear, so I'd appreciate some advice."

I figured the problem was out of my hands now. I fell asleep.

A man named Harry Thurman proved to be an angel of the Lord, but the man never knew it. He owned an ice-cream stand about fifteen miles down the highway from my motel. When he opened it up the next morning, his first two customers were Tarzan and Rex. They just came walking up to the stand and stuck their heads over the counter, and Mr. Thurman nearly jumped out of his shoes. He found some rope, tied them to a fence, and called the police.

The motel man drove me to where they were. I took a saddle and bridle along and rode Rex back to the motel, with Tarzan on a lead rope. It was a foolish thing to do, but I was too excited to think right. The rain was just a drizzle, and if I'd brought my gear along, why then we would have been fifteen miles closer to California. As it was, we had to go back over those same miles the next day. But you can't have everything, and I did have my horses back again, even if I didn't have common sense.

The next day was fair and we went five miles beyond the ice-cream stand. Now we were in a part of Arkansas that didn't have many houses. The few that we saw were big ones, where the owners of plantations lived. Not far from each house there'd be a cluster of cabins where the sharecroppers lived. It was rice growing country, mostly, and the air was filled with billions of gnats. I was told that mules working in the field sometimes died from gnats getting up their noses. For several days there, I found I had to chain-smoke cigarettes to keep the gnats away from our heads. Real cigarettes. Couldn't locate any sweet fern along there. All the smoking had me coughing real hard again, but there was no other way to lick those gnats. We were getting closer to the cypress swamps, and the closer we got, the thicker the bugs got.

I was never invited to stay over in the big houses, but five out of the first six nights from the motel the field bosses let me use empty cabins. They had only rice hay for the horses, so the corn I carried came in handy along that stretch of road. The one night I slept in a real house was at a goldfish farm. I thought the man and his wife were joking when they told me what they raised, but it was a fact. They shipped their fish to stores all over the country.

I made a note of one thing the goldfish farmer told me, because it sounded unusual enough to succeed. "I'm sitting on a million-dollar idea and nobody will listen. I think the sardine industry is afraid I'll run it out of business. Ever prepare little goldfish the way they do sardines? Well, I have, and they taste just as good, if not better. Furthermore, they make a more colorful and attractive dish. And you can raise goldfish cheaper than you can catch sardines! You don't even need boats."

So I told him about the canning companies in Maine. They're always looking for new ideas. "America is great because it has the courage to try new things," Uncle Waldo was fond of saying. "The radio, for instance, and the dial telephone."

It was a day beyond the goldfish farm that we started seeing the first small patches of swamp. Two days later, we were on the twelve-mile stretch of road that heads right through the biggest cypress swamp in the state. On each side of that road, as far as we could see, giant trees grew out of deep water. Some of the tree roots stuck out of the water like bent fingers, and they called those roots "knees" in that country.

They cut and polish those cypress knees and sell them as ornaments and lamp bases and such. Roadside stands make a living selling them. I was offered several knees for free, but never accepted. I didn't know if I'd ever again have a place for an ornament or a lamp, and the general idea was still to travel as light as possible anyway.

We didn't spot a single snake on the way through the swamp, but I breathed easier all the same once we reached the far side. A mile beyond, some folks asked me to stay the night with them. It was early, but I was ready to call it a day, for the temperature was in the eighties and the heat had sort of sapped my strength. They didn't have a barn, but that was all right in fair weather. I hitched the horses to a fence with feeding length ropes. They were on grass and I knew they'd be happy.

Next morning, the ropes were there but not the horses. During the night, somebody had untied Tarzan and Rex, but we never discovered who the guilty party was. The folks told me there hadn't been any horse stealing in these parts for a long time. They'd figured that some child had freed the horses, just for the fun of it.

The sheriff felt the same way. He kept telling me that only a fool would steal such well-known horses and that there were no fools in Arkansas.

"Maybe this fool came from another state," I suggested. I was plenty worried, but everybody else was as calm as a Maine cove on a still day.

"Now you just sit tight while I run back to the office," the sheriff said. "Wouldn't be surprised if somebody has already found them and phoned in. If not, I'll make a few phone calls to the west of here."

"What about the other directions?"

"All swamp. No horse in his right mind will go near that swamp."

Two hours later, he returned to tell me that my horses had been found on the far side of the swamp to the east. During the night, they had crossed back over the swamp

115

and turned up at the corral where they'd spent the night before.

The folks drove me to where the horses were, and then I rode Rex and led Tarzan back over the same twelve miles of swamp road. It was just another lost day: Plenty of travel, but not one inch of progress.

Next morning, when we moved away from the big swamp, the packs on the horses weighed a few pounds less. I'd left the heavy coat, all but one of the union suits, and the rest of my winter gear with the sheriff. I still looked like a tramp, but I was dressed in my balmy weather outfit: Army fatigue hat, cotton shirt, drill pants and real shoes. Now it was true spring, although the heat was worse than it gets to be most summers in Maine. The sheriff promised to hold my winter stuff and ship it on to me at a later date when I wanted it. I hoped I wouldn't have to face another winter, but there was no telling when the horses would decide to strand me somewhere. "From now on, I'm keeping a sharper eye on you two boys," I told them. I was on Rex at the time, and if he heard me, he didn't prick his ears. It seemed to me that he was more to blame for their escapades than Tarzan. That big bay was determined to get back to Tennessee. He was either homesick or lovesick.

He was in need of hind shoes again, and to make it easier on his feet we left the highway and plodded along an old, unused, dirt road that had once been the main route to a rice elevator and cleaning mill. It was supposed to save us time getting to the nearest blacksmith, but I had my doubts about that. So far, every short cut had proven out as the long way to anywhere.

They called it a dirt road, but it was mostly sand and dotted with puddles of water. It was slow going. The horses kept their heads down and watched where they stepped. I had nothing to do but sit in the saddle and admire the scenery, and I could have dozed, except for those darn gnats.

Depeche Toi was dashing in and out of the trees on each side of the road, and Tarzan was behind us at the end of a twenty-foot lead rope.

The other end of the lead rope was tied to my saddle ring, so when Tarzan stopped of a sudden, so did Rex. I looked back and yanked on the rope, but Tarzan wasn't about to budge. He was trembling, and when I turned Rex and walked back to him, the black one side-stepped to the edge of the road. I dismounted and walked to him, and then Depeche Toi was there, barking excitedly and pressing his quarters against my legs. I turned around to see what he was barking at, and there in the road was a coiled snake! I'd never seen a cottonmouth, but I knew I was looking at one. His mouth looked like it was stuffed with cotton. His real name is water moccasin, but under either name he's dangerous.

Tarzan was the only one with horse sense. He was as far away as he could get. Depeche Toi must have thought of himself as a mongoose. The dog continued to bark his fool head off, and he was crouched not two feet from the snake. Old cottonmouth was waving his head and spitting out his tongue. I was afraid that he'd strike out for the dog.

Then Rex got into the act. Calm as you please, the big bay swung around and planted his hind feet in a puddle that was no more than a foot from the snake.

Now mister cottonmouth was really swinging his head. He couldn't make up his mind about whether to strike at the horse, or the dog, or me. And while he was making up his mind, Rex lifted his right leg and kicked down and back. That sent a shower of muddy water and sand smack onto the snake. He uncoiled and slithered off into a gutter as fast as he could go. I grabbed Depeche Toi or he would have given chase.

When we reached the rice elevator, I told a fellow there about what had happened. He was inclined not to believe me and told me, "Either you've been drinking, or the horse stomped to get rid of the gnats. The horse hasn't been born who'll fight a snake. A horse and a snake are like a woman and a mouse. By the way, who told you to take this road?"

"The sheriff."

"He should have known better. Since it stopped being the main road, folks around here have called it Cotton Mouth Road."

"What's it like from here to Little Rock?"

"You won't see as many snakes, but the ones you do see will be bigger. They like to sun themselves on the hot surface of the road, so keep a sharp look ahead."

I paid strict attention to the road surface all afternoon, but the word must have been out that Rex was on his way. I didn't see another snake.

When we reached the outskirts of Little Rock, I was disappointed in the looks of the place. It didn't appear anywhere near the size Papa had described. He'd been there in 1922, too, checking on a hotel that was for sale. They wouldn't lower the price and he was broke anyway, but he always said he could have become rich in Little Rock.

The reason the city looked so small to me that afternoon was that we were in North Little Rock, or ten miles short of where I thought we were. Then I found out that the only stables were on the far side of the city, or about seventeen miles away. I was busy selling postcards and autographing them when somebody told me that. The disappointment must have showed on my face, for a young woman spoke right up with, "Don't worry. All of you are coming home with me."

Her name was Florence. Not Florence Nightingale, although that name would have fit her. She took complete charge of me and my friends and wouldn't let me lift a hand. She told the reporters just when they could interview me, gave directions to the photographers, lined up television and radio shows, drove me around to the Army surplus store so that I could stock up on pajamas and other things that wear out quickly, bought me some supplies for the road, and found the right smithy for Rex and told him not to charge,

Wherever we stopped around North Little Rock, people would gather and ask for my cards. Florence told each one what to pay; the richer a man looked, the more he had to pay. "The card is free, but you can't have the card without her autograph, and that costs fifty cents," she told the rich ones.

In the three days with Florence, cash on hand had increased by almost eighty dollars. The only dispute we had was over the route I planned to take: Up north across Missouri, then westward through Kansas to Colorado.

"You'll save hundreds of miles cutting through Oklahoma to Colorado. That's the way to go. Look at this map." She was just as sure of herself as the woman named Sam back in Pennsylvania, and the fact that I wanted to see Kansas made no sense to her. "Stay away from Kansas. It's not safe there for a woman alone. All those twisters and everything else. Promise me."

So I promised, or I wouldn't have had any sleep that last night. The last Florence saw of us the next morning, we were heading for Little Rock and on to Oklahoma. I planned to get the city between us by the next day, then forget Oklahoma and hurry north to Missouri.

But we never did get into the city. People kept delaying us and asking for cards. By nightfall we'd covered a bare six miles and now were in an area of fenced-in junk. A watchman told me there was plenty of clean grass at the far end of his yard, so we stayed there for the night. The dog and I were comfortable on a bed of old car seats, and Rex and Tarzan stayed hitched to the fence and munched green grass. In the morning we had to wait until somebody unlocked the gate. All night long we'd been locked in with all the other valuable junk.

Again we headed for the city. We'd covered less than a mile when some riders from the North Little Rock Riding Club came along. They'd been looking for us since dawn and wanted us to visit their club house. I accepted, thinking that the club house wasn't too far away.

Nobody mentioned that the club house was near Lake Conway, which was a full day's ride away to the north, or that I would be the guest of honor at the club's annual banquet and dance.

There were about twenty of us in the group, and we stopped just once for lunch in a picnic grove, and within minutes a truck arrived and some waiters jumped out of it and started serving food.

After that, we were on the road another six hours before we reached the club house. It was dark by then, but the whole outside was lit up by thousands of colored lights. There were hundreds of parked cars and hitched horses around the place. The club house must have been the biggest thing of its kind in America.

Some uniformed boys took charge of Tarzan and Rex, and that's the last I saw of them that night. Two fancy-dressed ladies escorted me and Depeche Toi to a suite of rooms that had been reserved for us, and there they asked me if I wanted to change to something fresh or not. When I explained that my other clothes were with my gear, one of them opened a closet door. Hanging in there were about a dozen beautiful gowns. "Pick your color," said the lady. "If it doesn't fit, we'll make it fit."

I was tempted to try a blue one, but I had come there as a lady tramp and somehow I felt I should remain one. "Never worn a fancy gown in my life, and I guess I never will," I told the ladies. "I thank you for your kindness, but I'd feel like a periwinkle out of the shell in one of those."

Then all of us, and Depeche Toi, went down to the main room where the banquet was already under full steam. Never saw so much food under one roof. There was enough there to feed everybody in Minot for a month or more. I had my first Maine lobster since Uncle Waldo lost his job with the W.P.A.

That was a wonderful party, and after the first few minutes I was able to adjust to the noise and understand what people were saying to me. The dance band played until long

Mesannie Wilkins, bound for California, leaves Maine riding Tarzan. Depeche Toi travels alongside, leashed to the saddle. Later, the dog rode much of the way aboard the horse.

Tarzan was impatient to "keep going," too. He is held by Mesannie while they are photographed during the trek from coast-to-coast.

Mrs. Wilkins atop Rex, who replaced Tarzan as her riding horse, Depeche Toi and Tarzan following.

Mesannie, Depeche Toi and a room clerk in the lobby of the once famous Highland Hotel in Springfield, Massachusetts. Dinner was served in Mrs. Wilkins' room.

The District Ranger in Canby, California points out a favorable route to Los Angeles.

Nearing their journey's end, Mesannie and her boys (Depeche Toi, Tarzan and Rex) arrive at Yuba City, California.

Tarzan, with Depeche Toi aboard, appears to be asking King a question. King was a gift from Art Linkletter. Mrs. Wilkin's often stopped long enough for admirers to take her picture.

Photo taken after her arrival in North Hollywood. Mrs. Wilkins, Depeche Toi, Tarzan and King. Tarzan made the entire trip from Maine to California but King replaced Rex about 180 miles from the destination.

Mesannie Wilkins appears on Art Linkletter's show,
in Hollywood with King.

CBS Photo by C

after midnight. It may not have been the best band in the world, but it was one of the loudest. Depeche Toi couldn't stand the racket, and he disappeared early. He stayed just long enough to sample about a hundred tidbits offered to him by the club members.

At midnight, things were quieted down while the club president made a speech. Then he introduced me as "The lady who is proving that the horse is here to stay." I'd met about everybody there by that time, so I just waved and didn't say anything. Then the president asked me to waltz with him. I did, and after that I waltzed with several other gentlemen, no matter what kind of a tune the band played. Not having waltzed in more than thirty-five years, I felt a little rusty, but all my partners said that I did fine.

It was four in the morning before everybody went home and I went upstairs to my rooms. Depeche Toi was sound asleep outside the door. I was just about able to keep my eyes open, and had no trouble falling to sleep once I hit the bed.

When I awakened, the sun was full in my face. It was one in the afternoon, and I'd never slept that late before when healthy. I washed and dressed, and hurried downstairs. They were cleaning up the main room, but the cook and some of his helpers served me a late breakfast in a little room to the side.

By three, we were on the road again and traveling north toward the Missouri line. I was afraid that Florence would come driving along and make us turn for Oklahoma, but that didn't happen. And some of the time I thought back to the night before. It had been sort of a New Year's Eve in the month of May. I regretted that I hadn't tried on that blue gown. It might have fit. And if it had, I would have been a better fit for the party.

He was a giant of a man, as tall as anyone I'd seen away from a carnival, and he stood in the middle of that Missouri road with arms outstretched, as if he meant to block our way. I was on Rex, and we stopped about twenty feet from the man and waited for him either to get out of the way or say something.

"Baby!" he said, loud and clear, and he walked toward us. "Baby, where have you been? I've been waiting for you."

I was pretty sure he wasn't talking to me. Then I was real sure, for he threw his arms around Rex's neck and kissed him on the nose. Next, he came around to the side and lifted me right out of the saddle. It was easy for him. He stood about seven feet. "Mom wants to meet you," he told me. "Come!"

We walked up a side road to his farm. The house looked as if it had never been painted, but the big, red barn was in prime condition. You could tell the man took good care of his animals.

Mom was almost as tall as her son. Not far from my own age, but not a gray hair on her head. I must have looked like a puny midget to her. When I went into the house to meet her, she seemed to be very unfriendly. She just stared at me for a minute, then pointed to a chair by the kitchen table. After I sat down, she brought a long loaf of bread to the table. Then she poured some salt on a piece of paper and sat down opposite me.

While I watched, Mom tore off a hunk of bread, sprinkled salt on it, and started eating. Without saying a word, I did the same. I figured that was the right thing to do, and it was. Back in Maine, when I was in the homes of strangers, I always did as they did.

We sat there about five minutes, each taking a turn at the bread, until we'd eaten the whole loaf. After that, Mom smiled and said, "You stay here tonight. Welcome."

It was early afternoon and I wanted to push on, but it didn't seem smart to argue with people that size. So we stayed the night there, and the son took wonderful care of my friends. The man and his mother didn't talk much, but whenever they said anything, they made every word count. Scandinavians, I thought.

Postcard business was poor all through the Ozarks. People knew who I was and talked to me, but they seldom asked for the cards. Still, they were helpful judging distances for me and telling me where I could find a place to stay. It was hard for me to judge just how many miles we could cover in the up-and-down country, but when someone told me, "You can make twenty miles easy before dark, and you'll find a good stable there," then the stable was always waiting for us at dusk. Sometimes we'd make only eight or ten miles, but we'd always find the stable or the hotel right where it was supposed to be.

Folks call them hills down there, but I knew hills, and those that we went over were mountains. Often there would be a cliff on one side of the road and nothing but space on the other, and sometimes the road was a trifle narrow. It was just that way one afternoon when a car came toward us and stopped where the road broadened a bit. Two men got out of the car and walked over to us.

"We're from Marshfield," one said to me. "You can see it down in the valley there. All those roofs. The town is about three miles from this spot, if you could fly."

"If this road gets any narrower, I may be forced to do just that," I told him.

"Except for one little stretch, you've got nothing to worry about. Must have been a rock fall there this morning. We were just able to squeeze through in the car. I'd suggest you lead your horses along there, and be sure to crowd the hill side. Say, that dog of yours is going to be flying before he knows it!"

Depeche Toi was trotting back and forth on the outside edge of the road. He was living dangerously, and showing off at the same time. I called to him, but he crouched and stuck his head over the rim before he decided to come. I figured the look downhill had scared him.

123

"This is a windy road and you've got about eight more miles of it before you come to Marshfield. That should be about six o'clock. Now, when you get to the outskirts, look for a yellow car. Mrs. Murphy from the Chamber of Commerce will be in it. She'll show you where the stable is and then take you to her house. You'll be staying over in Marshfield for several days."

The men got back into their car and waited until we were past them. Then they drove off in the opposite direction. I don't know just how they got back to Marshfield, but we didn't see them again that day. And the "one little stretch" of bad road up ahead turned out to be about a half mile long. The packs on the horses extended out about eighteen inches on each side, so we didn't have too much room to spare. It didn't seem possible that the car had squeezed through there, but it had, somehow. I led both horses and kept Tarzan, who was naturally slower, out front. It was downgrade, and he had the sense to go slower than usual. But not Rex. He was all for going faster, and kept trying to turn out. So I let Tarzan proceed on his own and kept myself at Rex's head until we were well by the danger stretch. They didn't have a rail anywhere along that road. A drunken driver would have had to be pretty drunk before trying that road.

Sure enough, it was just about six when we reached the outskirts of Marshfield and the lady in the yellow car. Her name was Dot Murphy, and she told me that I needed a rest, whether I knew it or not. "And even if you don't need it," she added, "your horses do. Going up and down in the Ozarks is hard on any horse, if he's not used to it."

So I was the town's guest for three days, during which time I didn't get any large amounts of rest. They had me speak at luncheons and a school assembly; I was interviewed by both the press and the radio; I went on a garden club tour, and I umpired the first inning of a baseball game between little boys. The Chamber of Commerce had my laundry done for me, and Mrs. Murphy embroidered MESANNIE

124

across the back of my grey moleskin shirt, so that people didn't have to ask what my first name was. Also, a grain store there took pictures of Rex selecting a bag of grain from thousands of bags. The bags were stacked in piles, and he picked out a bottom one. We left the store with that bag and several more, as much as Rex and Tarzan could carry.

There was a big shower on the morning we left Marshfield, and the day cleared hot. When we reached Ash Grove that night, all four of us were tuckered out. It didn't help any to find out that the town was as different from Marshfield as day and night. I couldn't locate a stable, and nobody with a barn wanted to put us up. So we headed on through to open country, then pulled off the road and made camp for the first time on the journey. After graining the horses heavy, I hitched them to a cattle gate where the grass was thick. Then I fed the dog and thought about feeding myself, but didn't. I was just too tuckered.

My bed was a blanket which I spread over a thick mat of oak leaves. But there were too many rocks under the leaves, and I had to shift the blanket around several times before I found a more or less comfortable spot. After that, it took less time for the chiggers to find me. Each one bit like ten. Finally, I had to roll up in a blanket and hope for the best. Then I did fall asleep, but not for too long: About fifty cows arrived on the other side of the cattle gate and started talking to my horses. Our campsite was alongside the fencing of one of the biggest cow pastures in Missouri. All night long, more cows kept arriving and mooing their greetings, and their music wasn't a lullaby to my ears. Back in Maine, I'd read about the joys of sleeping under the western sky, and I'd looked forward to doing just that, but there wasn't even a single joy for me that night. When dawn came, I couldn't recall when I'd been so tired so early in the day. The horses were frisky as kittens when we broke camp, but I was mad as a hornet, and came close to throwing Missouri rocks at Missouri cows.

It was another hot day for all of us, and a hot-itchy day

for me in particular. My blanket roll hadn't discouraged those chiggers! Their after-effects were worse than the gnats down in Arkansas. Those tiny-winged things had been impartial, but the chiggers hadn't bothered with the dog or the horses.

On up the road near Nevada, and that was a town—not the state—a woman invited us to stay at her home. Her big, front yard was unmowed, which might have been the reason for the invitation: Tarzan and Rex mowed the green grass for her. When I told her about the chiggers, she said, "I hope you won't be dead by morning."

"What makes you think I might be?" I asked.

"Well we call them ticks, and some ticks are deadly poisonous. Would you like some more coffee?"

"Maybe I'd better find a doctor."

"No, it's too late for a doctor now. We'll just have to wait and see. Were you near any sheep?"

"Just cows," I told her. "Just cows that were too dumb to sleep."

"Well, we won't worry too much, then. The poisonous ticks are mostly found around sheep."

She gave me some stuff to put on the bites. It was supposed to relieve the itching, but it didn't help much. I slept soundly anyway, and in the morning I awakened to find myself still alive.

"I wouldn't sleep on the ground anymore, if I were you," the woman told me at breakfast. "We have plenty of snakes, too, this time of year."

Nobody else in Missouri had mentioned snakes to me. I hadn't seen any, and I knew the land wasn't wet enough for cottonmouth. So I just had to figure that the woman was one of those who had run scared all her life and imagined all sorts of dangers. Maybe that's why she didn't find a husband.

I found stables on the next four nights, so I didn't worry about ticks or snakes. And I didn't change my mind about the woman until the fifth night away. That was near Har-

126

risonville, where an elderly farmer told me we could use his barn. I put all the gear in a big, empty stall, and made a bed out of blankets over hay before going to the house to meet the farmer's wife and have supper.

"Mother will be right along," the farmer said. "Your bed is nearly ready. We've set it up, and she's attending to the bedding."

I told him that wasn't necessary, that I'd planned to sleep in the barn. I assumed his wife was elderly, too, and I didn't want to be a burden. She proved to be older than he was.

"Mrs. Wilkins wants to sleep in the barn," he told her.

"You will not sleep in the barn!" she said to me. "Father killed a little rattler in that empty stall just this morning, and rattlers always go in pairs. This one was only three feet or so, but the mate might be bigger."

I slept in the house that night and tried my best not to be a burden. They were spry for elderly people anyway.

The days were hot and the nights were cold, but the real problem was water. That section was going through a drought, and people with cattle had to haul water long distances. We were lucky. Most gas stations were happy to give us water, but the stations were few and far apart.

Eighty miles or so below Kansas City, we found our first water in seven hours, at a gas station in a little village. "How did you get this far?" the man asked. "You were supposed to turn off two miles back. For three days now, Mrs. Tuttle has been telling everybody to tell you to come to her place. She had the best pasture around here, and only one old pet horse. Best driven well, too. Plenty of water."

He told me how to get to the Tuttle place. It meant an extra five miles going and coming, but we were ten miles from the nearest stable and I wasn't about to camp out again in Missouri if I could help it.

As we started off, the station man came running after us.

He said, "I might as well tell you something. I'm new around here myself, so all I know is what people say, but Mrs. Tuttle is supposed to be a little tetched. So watch your step."

She looked like any other normal old lady to me. About my height and maybe twenty years older, but very thin. She couldn't have weighed more than seventy pounds. "I'm so glad you came," she said. "You must be starved. I'll start supper while you take care of your horses. Just put your things in the barn. Oh, bring all your blankets in when you come."

Later, Mrs. Tuttle folded all my blankets and laid them one on top of the other on a thick rug in her front room. "My husband used to fix it this way," she explained. "He always used to say that when folks are used to camping they can never get a good night's sleep in a bed. I have plenty of beds upstairs, if you'd prefer one, but they have springs, and I know you like something hard. Do Maine people sleep outdoors all of the time?"

"I've known a few who don't."

"My husband would have liked you. He was a man of great courage, just as you are a woman of great courage. Oh, he did know horses, too. Horses and hunting were his life. And he loved dogs. Do you mind if your dog sleeps with me? Our dogs always slept on our bed."

So I slept on the floor that night, and Depeche Toi slept on her bed. I don't know where she thought Maine dogs slept when they were camping.

She was up and had a big breakfast ready for me before dawn. "I know how it is with you outdoor people," she said. "The daylight hours are so precious. I've fixed some lunch for you to take. And I wish I had a tent to give you. You really should have a tent. The West is different than the East. There'll be times when you won't find a dry place to camp, and this nice weather won't last forever. What about the Rocky Mountains? You'll need something to wear in the mountains at night. I have just the thing!"

The "thing" she gave me came in handier sooner than I expected. It was a heavy parka with a fur-trimmed hood that had belonged to her husband. You pulled it over your head, and there were slits in each side to stick your hands in over your chest. It was much too big for me, but I didn't know how to refuse it without offending Mrs. Tuttle, especially after she said, "My husband would want you to have it."

Well, that parka came in handy on the night we neared Raytown, a suburb of Kansas City, Missouri. Black clouds had been forming all afternoon, and now the thunder rumbled and the rain came fast. We pulled into a gas station and I asked where I could find shelter for the four of us.

"You'll drown before you get to the nearest stable," the man told me. "But there's a church up the road with a field on this side of it. Go to the rear of that field and you'll find a shed where the preacher used to keep his mules. There's a steep bank behind it that goes down to a creek that's mostly dry now, but maybe this rain will put some water into it for the horses."

In that smart, heavy rain, the tall grass and bushes made the field seem like a jungle. When we found the shed, Rex and Tarzan wanted no part of it. It had housed mules and was beneath their dignity.

I didn't argue with them. I tore the gear from their backs and put it into the old shed. If the boys didn't want to stay dry, that was their business. I was wet to the skin, but I intended to at least sleep on something dry that night, so I put the blankets down on the dirt floor of the shed the same way Mrs. Tuttle had put them down on the rug in her front room.

When the rain let up, I grained the horses and then hitched them to a wire fence. After that, I told Depeche Toi to guard the gear and I set off to find some hot food for myself. All my clothes were wringing wet, and I felt chilled, so I wore the heavy parka. It was the only dry thing on me.

I found a little restaurant about a half-mile away and

had a supper of beef stew, pie and coffee. The owner knew who I was, and when I left he gave me a bag of half-picked steak bones for Depeche Toi. As I started back for the church field, the thunder sounded again, and by the time I got to the gas station the rain was so thick I could hardly see.

"Get in here quick!" the station man yelled. "This is a ring-tailed peeler!"

I didn't need a second invitation. The man told me I'd best stay there all night, but I was anxious to get the food to Depeche Toi and move the horses into some tree shelter. So when the rain slackened at about midnight, I headed back to my boys.

I could hear Rex calling out, and I ran the last hundred feet. He had caught his halter in the wire, in such a way that he could neither feed nor lie down. Judging from the way the ground was pawed, he'd been caught for a long time. I freed him, then led both horses into a grove of trees and hitched them there. Now Depeche Toi was barking, just as if he knew I was carrying bones for him. Actually, he was announcing sad news: In my absence, the creek had overflowed its banks and flooded the shed floor, and now all the gear was wet, and the blankets were soggy.

So it was back to the gas station for me, and I spent the night there in the office. The place was heated, but business was so good the door was open a good deal of the time. It was dry there, but hardly warm. "Do people buy gas all night long around these parts?" I asked.

"No," said the night man. "It's just heavy tonight because of the holiday. In case you don't know it, Memorial Day is now one hour old. But business will die down in an hour or so, and then we'll stay warm. You see that safe there by you?"

I didn't. All I saw was a small steel door on the floor. It was no bigger than my hand. He came over to it, opened it, and pushed a wad of paper money into it. "The money drops through a pipe into the safe down below," he explained. "I don't dare keep more money out than I need for change. Lots of robberies around here. See that sign on the wall?"

It was a big, printed sign and it read—THE NIGHT MAN DOES NOT KNOW THE COMBINATION OF THE SAFE.

"And that's the truth," he said. "Being alone, I might be scared into telling. Of course, some of those fellows don't believe what they read. They beat up the night man anyway."

He told me that robbers usually worked in threes. One stayed in the car, one went to the wash room while the car was being gassed, and one came into the office while the night man changed a big bill. Then Mr. Wash Room came out and they had the night man two to one. "I can tell you that I'm worried tonight, with so much money coming in," he added.

I sat on the floor with my back to the wall and to one side of the door. Whenever the door opened, it sort of hid me from view, but I'd stand up anyway so that customers wouldn't think I was a drunken bum. After awhile, when business slackened, I managed to doze.

So I was sort of half asleep when a horn blew outside, and I was just on my feet and leaning against the wall when the door opened and a man came into the office. He hurried across it and into the wash room. Then in came the night man to change a bill, and a customer was with him. As soon as the cash register bell sounded, the first man popped out of the wash room and stepped behind the night man. I was standing behind the door, mostly hidden from view, and the two strangers hadn't noticed me.

I didn't have robbery on my mind. I'd forgotten all that the night man had told me, and wanted to see only if the rain had stopped. So I stepped out from behind the door. The strangers looked at me as if I had horns. My hands were inside the parka, the hood was up, and I suppose I looked like the devil himself. One of the strangers grabbed the change, and then both of them ran out of the door. They hopped into a car and off they went.

"You deserve a medal," the night man said. "They thought you were carrying a gun in that parka."

"All I deserve is sleep," I told him. I sat down and went to sleep. Hours later, when I awoke, the sun was shining, and the station boss was there and telling the night man that a gas station about five miles away had been robbed during the night, and that the attendant there had been badly beaten.

We spent all of Memorial Day there in Raytown, using natural sunshine and a sterno heater to dry out the wet gear. Even the grain was soaked and swollen, but Rex and Tarzan didn't mind.

We reached Kansas City the next afternoon. I'd given that city as my next forwarding address, and it was a wonder that the mail was at the right post office: Nobody had told me that Kansas City is really two cities in two different states, one right next to the other, except for the bridge over the river.

I picked up quite a stack of mail and then started hunting for a stable. I found several, but none would have us. We had hit there at a time when horse distemper was running wild. Finally, a policeman directed me to Benjamin Stables at Hickman Mills, which was almost back to Raytown, the place we had left that morning. We had gained four miles while going twenty-seven.

A woman who was at the stable took me home with her to Raytown and that was my headquarters for the next few days. Mr. Benjamin, who owned the stables, located a fine blacksmith for me. I had new shoes put on all around and also spent some time shopping for a pup tent, tent pegs, canned heat and a few other needed articles. The newspapers took pictures of us, and I had a new cut made of the four of us. All in all, I treated money as if it grew on trees. It was all outgo and ran close to a hundred dollars. A little over two dollars remained, although I had bought only essentials.

I was shocked at what I had done, and decided to get back on the road before we were dead broke.

Then we ran into a real snag. Because of the horse distemper epidemic, the law wouldn't let us stop overnight in either of the Kansas Cities. Getting through both of them would have been at least a two-day trip for us.

A television station tried to help us by running our picture under the heading, "Who's Got a Truck?"

People phoned in with offers to truck us, and Mr. Benjamin was among the first. That same day, he trucked us through Kansas City, Missouri and over the bridge through Kansas City, Kansas and on into open country. By sundown, we were plodding along the highway in the general direction of Topeka.

For the first time since leaving Maine, I felt completely at home. It may have been because Kansas was the state where the term "saddle tramp" originated.

8   KANSAS—COLORADO

Back in the era of great cattle drives, Kansas was so full of drifting cowboys—some homeward bound, some looking for work, and others looking for trouble—that it became known as The State of Saddle Tramps. Now a Maine saddle tramp had come along.

Those first few days, people smiled and waved as they drove past us, but very few stopped to talk and buy post-cards. More and more we were hearing such shouts as "See you in Cheyenne!" Everybody seemed to assume that we'd get there in time for the big parade that sets off Frontier Days Week and the big rodeo. I wanted to see that rodeo, but I wasn't so sure we'd make it. At the time, I'd set our course southwest for Topeka, and Cheyenne was to the northwest. It just seemed to be the thing to do.

The official invitation to the Cheyenne affair had been in the stack of mail at Kansas City. There'd been an invitation from the rodeo people in Pendleton, Oregon, too, but we had no chance of making that one on time. We could have trucked there, of course, and the officials would have paid for that, but it would seem like cheating.

I still hadn't answered the rodeo people in either city, but I planned to the next time we put up at a motel, where high class stationery didn't cost anything. However, the bank roll was too low for a motel just then. The cards weren't moving too well.

Answering my mail had become quite a problem, and it was getting bigger every day. I could have used a secretary. By Kansas, two saddle bags were stuffed with envelopes carrying names and addresses of people from all over the country who had written to invite me to their homes, or to ask questions, or just to wish me luck. And then there were important letters, ones that deserved replies right away, but somehow I'd neglected them, too: Mrs. Sawyer of the newspaper in Lewiston, Maine, asking for news of my journey; Sam Hollis back in White Horse, Pennsylvania, telling me to turn around and make my home with her; Mrs. Bryar, the lady with the sled dogs in Massachusetts, offering to send me more folders at any time; and the sheriff in Arkansas, who was holding my winter clothes in a box at the jail, wanting to know what he should do now that somebody had stolen the box.

I was thinking about him when we made camp by the side of the highway that first night in Kansas. "Boys," I said to the horses, "somebody tried to steal you in Arkansas near that big swamp, and now somebody has stolen my clothes. But the sheriff was right: They don't have horse thieves down there, just old winter-clothes thieves."

Our camp site had been suggested by a friendly truck driver. "Just get on the other side of the ditch. Plenty of green grass there for your horses. Now don't get too far from the road. I'll pass the word along and we'll all keep an eye on you."

Those truck drivers passed the word from one to another in a hurry. All night long, trucks slowed down as they passed us, and the drivers tooted their horns. We were thirty feet from the road, but some of those horns tooted so loud that I was afraid the trucks were going to run right over me.

135

Other nights, we pitched camp at a greater distance from the road. The drivers always knew where we were, but the toots weren't close enough to keep me awake. What did keep me awake sometimes were the people who wanted to take our pictures. As I'd be unpacking about dusk, they'd stop their cars and come running our way with their cameras. Some even had flash bulbs. The nights were warm, but I didn't dare wear pajamas, for fear a bulb would pop while I was undressing. I suppose the pup tent would have been some protection, but I didn't pitch it on the way to Topeka. There was no trouble with the weather or ticks, and I didn't see any snakes.

On the night before we reached Topeka, we pulled off the road and I was just unloading the gear when a police car stopped and an officer got out of it. "What do you think you're doing?" he asked.

"I'm camping here."

"Well, now, I've heard that Maine people are stubborn, but you beat them all. Why are you camping here?"

"Do I need a permit?" I asked.

"No, but you are now in civilized country. The Topeka Motel has been holding a room for you all day. Didn't you get the invitation?"

It was news to me, and proved once again that Somebody was looking out for me. Now traveling in the wrong direction for Cheyenne made sense: I'd done it in order to acquire quality stationery I didn't have the money to buy.

Oh, I got the message. And I wrote more letters that one night than I'd written in any year of my life.

The motel's owners treated this tramp as if she were a queen. I sort of held court there—meeting all the other guests, talking to people who dropped in from the city, and being interviewed by reporters. A woman gave me two dollars to buy beer for Depeche Toi, but I bought him ice cream. And I set a one-day record for selling postcards.

136

When we left Topeka, I had thirty-two dollars in my pocket. That was the very same amount we had started with back in Minot, Maine almost eight months before. I tried to find some meaning in that and failed. Uncle Waldo would have found something.

We headed northwest for Cheyenne, but I didn't have any real hope that we'd get there in time for the big parade. To birds, Cheyenne was four hundred miles away. To us, it had to be much more than that, and we had about thirty days to cover whatever the mileage would be. I set our goal at fifteen miles a day, but figured to do better than that, since it was easy going for the boys. The countryside was real flat, and road grades were so gradual that you could go miles before a slight rise cut off the rear view. As far as the eye could see, sunflowers and weeds covered the landscape.

The days had been hot and the nights warm, but now, at the start of July, the nights turned suddenly cold, and there was plenty of dew on the ground in the morning. That's how it was the first night out from Topeka, and my off-and-on cough became a regular thing during the next day. When we stopped off at a stable in a town named Manhattan, I owned a pesky cold and was sweating like a trooper. The man there had to unload the horses for me. I felt too dizzy to do anything but sit on a box and watch him.

"Have you had mumps?" he asked me.

"I don't know. Why, is my face swollen?"

"No, but you sure look like you should lie down and get some rest. The reason I asked is that my kids have mumps. I was going to ask you into the house, but maybe you better stay in the stable."

I had no appetite, and didn't bother to feed myself. Later, I spread my blankets over bales of straw and used that for a bed. It was healthier than sleeping on the ground, as I'd done for so many nights in Kansas, but it didn't make me any healthier. By morning, I knew I was sick and I was more than a little scared: The doctor back in Maine had warned me that I'd always be an easy mark for pneumonia, having had it the winter before. So when the stableman arrived, I asked where I could find a doctor.

"Two miles down the road at the clinic," he told me. "You can't miss it. I'll saddle the big horse for you."

He did, and I managed to climb into the saddle and ride Rex to the clinic. They were the longest two miles in Kansas and then, at the clinic, I found that all the doctors were out of town at a convention. "They won't be back until Monday," the receptionist explained.

"I can't wait that long," I said, and then I had a coughing fit.

She bawled me out for not taking care of myself, and for not having seen a doctor before that morning. When she was through, I asked where the nearest doctor was.

"There are just a few others in town, but you can't see any one of them without an appointment," she said. And that was the truth. I went to three doctors and never got to see a single one. I had a terrible time climbing back aboard Rex each time, and I wouldn't have seen the stable again if the horse hadn't found his way back there without guidance from me.

When we got there, I was just able to get to the floor and stagger over to my bed on the straw. Depeche Toi came over to me and started whining. The stableman had been talking to a lady all the while. Now he came over to ask what the doctor had said.

"Couldn't find a doctor who would see me," I said.

Then the lady, who was there to rent a horse, came over to ask what was wrong.

"She can't find a doctor who will tend to her," said the man. "How do you like that? This poor woman is dying and she's a citizen of the United States, and no doctor will help her!"

"Are you the woman from Maine?" she asked.

"Just barely," I told her. "If I don't see a doctor, I won't be from anywhere."

"Now don't move," she said. "I'll find a doctor for you."

138

Her husband was a state trooper. She phoned him, and he arrived in about ten minutes.

"I'll tell you something," the trooper said to his wife and the stableman. "The next time you see somebody who needs a doctor and you can't find a doctor, call the hospital. That's where I'm taking this woman. Now let's get her into my car."

At the hospital, the doctor shot something into my arm and gave me a supply of pills. "You'll feel better in a few hours and much better in the morning," he predicted. "But you'll also need some rest. Don't travel for ten days."

"I'll never make Cheyenne in time," I complained.

"Yes, you will. But not this year. Next year."

I didn't feel like my old self the next morning, but I did feel so much better that I decided to take to the road right away.

"You won't go very far with the big bay," the stableman told me. "He needs new hind shoes."

Most horses went unshod in that part of Kansas, and the nearest blacksmith was an Army man at Fort Riley, a hundred miles away. Whenever the stable had a few horses to be shod, it was possible to get the smithy over, but he had to be notified a couple of weeks in advance.

It looked like the doctor was right about our getting to Cheyenne next year. But I took a chance and phoned Fort Riley and talked to the blacksmith. He came over that afternoon, shoed Rex and didn't charge a cent.

When I told him he should charge something for all his trouble, he grinned and said, "My great aunt would kill me. She's your mother's old friend, and your friend, too— Mrs. Annie Williams of Minot. The one who encouraged you to take this trip. She wrote me all about it. I'll bet you wouldn't have left Minot to try this, if she hadn't convinced you that you could do it."

I didn't have the heart to tell him that he was wrong, and that his great aunt had been the one who'd called me crazy and tried to make me stay at home. The only help that woman had ever given me was accidental and right then and there in Manhattan: Free shoes for Rex.

Clay Center and the Republican River were two days up ahead. The way I was feeling—weak and with dizzy spells— I wanted as smooth a ride as possible. So when we started off from Manhattan, I was aboard Rex.

That horse knew something was wrong with me. He stopped right quick when the dizziness hit me and I slumped forward and grabbed his mane. Then he just stood there waiting for me to do something.

What I did, was to loop a stout strap around the front of the saddle and fasten it through my belt. I was a little afraid of blacking out all the way and falling, and I figured the strap would at least keep me in the saddle.

It worked out that way. Whenever the dizziness hit, I'd slump and Rex would stop, but I didn't fall out of the saddle. He wouldn't move ahead unless I was sitting proper. Of course, the other boys knew something was going on, too. Tarzan and the dog didn't cause any trouble that day.

Along about noon, we pulled up before a lunch place. I wanted some hot nourishment, but the ground seemed a long way down, even with Rex stretching. So I just sat there atop him until the lunch man came walking out of his place. He had nothing else to do, there being no business. "Lost?" he asked.

"Not if this is the road to Clay Center."

"It is and you're lost. I saw you going by over an hour ago. Right now, you're headed for Manhattan."

That's when I knew I had blacked out at least once, although I had no memory of it. Somehow, Rex had turned himself around. I didn't know how many miles we had lost.

"Are you sure you know where you're going?" asked the man.

"I do, but the trouble is that my friends don't. Do you think I could have some hot soup out here?"

"Plenty of tables inside."

"I like to eat in the saddle. Saves time."

He brought the soup in a mug, and while I was drinking it he told me there'd be no charge and asked me things about Maine. The soup was lukewarm, but I didn't complain. It tasted good.

When he asked for a postcard, all I had to do was reach into the bag on Rex's right shoulder where I carried a supply along with the sterno heater and some dishes. The man wouldn't take the card for free. He insisted that I take a dime, and also some free advice:

"Not many places to stay between here and Clay Center. Pretty lonely road for somebody in the best of health, and you look like you belong in a hospital bed. I notice you got yourself lashed onto the saddle. Why not rest here for a few days? There's an empty trailer out back."

I told him that I was feeling better by the minute and couldn't lose any more time feeling sorry for myself. He turned Rex around for me and for the second time that day we headed down the highway for Clay Center.

We walked along all afternoon. Then I found a grassy site well off the highway and started to unpack the gear. Some cars stopped and several people crossed the field and stood around watching me. They were pleasant, but none offered to help me. A woman had a movie camera and two of the men had regular cameras, and they took pictures of us as I staggered around unpacking, taking off the saddles, and graining the horses.

Finally, when I just had to sit down, the camerawoman said, "We'd just love to get some pictures of you getting your horses ready for the road, too. Would you mind packing just one of the horses for us, please?"

I was too tuckered to even lift my head to look at her, but I did manage to say, "Lady, these are union horses, they've put in an eight-hour day, and I can't afford overtime."

"Did you hear that?" she asked the others. They left as a group and went back to their cars. I supposed they were tourists, and I knew they thought that I was being inconsiderate.

At dusk, Depeche Toi and I had a supper of army rations from cans we had carried all the way from New Hampshire. I'd saved them for an emergency, and now we had one. Hot food would have been better for me, but getting the heater started seemed like too much trouble. I didn't pitch the pup tent that night or the next few nights under the stars, and thanked the Lord for the absence of rain, ticks and snakes. The only risk I ran was rolling off my blankets while I slept. That put me in direct contact with a creeping species of cactus that grew everywhere on the Kansas ground. More than once my hands, feet and ankles got covered with irritating, tiny spines that were hard to find.

It took us an extra day to make Clay Center, and two days instead of one to make Beloit. The dizzy spells kept recurring, although with less frequency, and I didn't black out again. Still, I kept myself fastened to the saddle on top of Rex, just in case.

Without me as part of his load, Tarzan thought he was on vacation and started acting frisky. We were passing through wheat country where the road was straight and wide, but we had to keep to the side because of heavy truck traffic and big wheat combines. Those combines had cranelike arms that swept over us as they passed by, and they frightened Tarzan. He'd rear back and dance until we were clear of those arms, and it was a wonder that his pack straps held. I kept waiting for him to spill the gear all over the road, but it didn't happen. The way those big trucks roared by, anything spilled would have been flattened flatter than a johnny cake.

Apart from the wheat in the fields, the only things growing along the way were wild lettuce, thistles and ragweed. So a touch of hay fever added to my miseries. Also, for a few days there, I thought we'd all die of thirst. Homes were far apart and well back from the road; we couldn't reach ground

142

water that we saw because of the endless miles of wire fences. I didn't know then that the wire could be untwisted without slacking a whole fence, and nobody told me until we reached Beloit, where my informer was a woman who treated the horses to a stable and took me and the dog home with her. It was my first night in a bed since Topeka. That bed and a hot bath had me feeling much better.

The woman's name was Louise Shilling, and I thought maybe we were distantly related until she told me she was only fourth generation American. "But there are other Shillings in Kansas," she told me, "and some of them may be in your family line. There are at least two families in Norton, and one near Oberlin. Then there used to be a Walter Shilling in Phillipsburgh. Was your Uncle Waldo's name Walter?"

She knew we were headed through all those towns, which is why she mentioned them in particular. And Waldo, as I told her, stood for Waldo and nothing else. The eldest son in a Libby family was always named Waldo. My uncle used to tell people that Waldo meant "Well Done" in Gaelic, but he'd chuckle when he told it.

All the Shillings I'd ever known were inquisitive people, and that woman in Beloit was not an exception. She asked all sorts of questions, and wanted to know why we didn't travel at night when it would be cooler for us.

"Because the first night might be our last one," I explained. "The way the cars and trucks speed on the roads in these parts, we'd be nothing but memories in short order."

She hadn't thought of that, and then she said something that hadn't crossed my mind: "I've been talking with my friends, and we think that you'll end up in the movies."

I laughed at the time, and the more I thought about it, the funnier it seemed. It was a pleasant pastime to think about being a movie star, and in the course of the next few days—as we walked along the bank of the Solomon River toward Phillipsburg—I got into the habit of saying things like, "Boys, when we get to California, we'll pay a visit to

143

the movie people. I'll dress up in a skirt and sweater and a big, white hat." Other times, I'd say, "Don't laugh, boys, because we might make it big. Did Tom Mix or Hoot Gibson or William S. Hart ever ride horseback coast to coast? Why, I've spent more time in the saddle on this trip than they did in all their lives."

It was all day-dreaming, of course, but it helped to pass the time. There were long stretches in Kansas with nobody to talk to. Not that people in Kansas were unfriendly: Much of the time, they just weren't around.

All along the road from Maine, whenever reporters asked me what I intended to do after reaching California, I'd been saying that I planned on getting a job taking care of cows or hogs. Now, the very next time I was asked, I intended to say that I planned on getting into the movies. I even picked out a screen name for myself: Mesannie Hart. That was in honor of William S. Hart, Uncle Waldo's favorite hero. "There's nobody around today who could touch him," my uncle told me a thousand times. "He never said much, but you knew he was a good man all the way through. His nose was almost as big as yours."

Still, when the first reporter in Phillipsburg put the question to me, I said, "I aim on getting a job taking care of cows or hogs." The word "aim" came out naturally, as if I was already a western star.

We camped in a park on the far side of the town that night. The spot had good, green grass and stand-pipe-water faucets, so it was ideal for the horses. It would have been a nice place to stay for a few days, but I wanted to see at least some of that rodeo in Cheyenne.

I was just fixing the straps on Tarzan's load the next morning when I heard a man say, "Hello, there!" I turned and found myself facing a regular tramp. He had a dirty blanket roll on his back and a stubble of beard on his face.

"I saw you going into the park last night," he said. "Just the horses' rumps, and thought it was some kids. If I'd known it was you, I would have come over and stayed with you. Where are you going today?"

"Norton."

"Same here. Do you know where you're stopping tonight? I'll join you."

"At a motel," I told him. I figured he couldn't get into one, but I might, in an emergency.

The police always told me to camp close to well traveled roads. They knew a car or truck would come along, in case I needed help. Now I knew why they had never recommended parks.

We were running low on postcards again by the time we reached Norton, Kansas. Getting them printed with the new cut showing Rex meant a three-day delay, but we had to have those cards. The income from them was our only means of support.

For three days running, the heat had been over one hundred degrees, and shade was hard to come by. On that day near Norton, we hadn't seen a single tree. All we'd seen in the wheat land were thousands of acres of wheat and millions of sunflowers and weeds.

But I was thankful for the heat and the lack of shade. The sun had baked my ailments right out of me. I felt so healthy that I decided to put up my tent when we made camp on the outskirts of town. But the wooden pegs wouldn't hold in the sandy soil.

A reporter came along to interview me, and he helped drive the pegs snug into the ground. It was getting onto dusk when he was through asking questions, and the last one was, "What will you do as soon as I leave?"

"Take care of my boys, then feed myself, then curl up in the pup tent and fall asleep," I told him.

"Just take care of your boys," he said. "We have a surprise for you."

The surprise came along in a truck just as I was about to put the coffee on the heater. A caterer had sent out three men to serve me a hot supper. They even brought along a table and a chair. The supper was more like a one-person banquet, and I sure enjoyed it. I sat down in the glare of the truck's headlights and stuffed myself. There was too much food for just me, so Depeche Toi, who had already eaten, found the room to take care of the extras. He slept most of the next day.

Toward late afternoon on the second day, a young woman arrived with a hot supper that she had prepared herself. She brought along a folding table and two folding chairs, set everything up and served. So we had supper together there in the field. I was her guest, but she acted as if she was the guest, and I did most of the talking. I thought she was forty or so, but she wouldn't tell me her age, or her name, or even if she was from Norton.

"Who I am doesn't mean anything," she said. "We may never see each other again. You see, I don't have much longer to live."

I told her my doctor had told me the same thing, but not to give up, because doctors don't always know everything.

"They know," she insisted.

"It took sixty-three years and this trip to teach me one thing," I told her. "Most things in life are foreordained, or I wouldn't be here telling you this. With all due credit to doctors, some don't know what's foreordained and what isn't."

I didn't know if my words of wisdom helped the poor woman or not, but they helped me. I was far from Maine and still alive, and willing to believe almost anything.

Next day, we picked up the new postcards, paid for same, sold a few, and started for the town of Oberlin on Sappa Creek. It was still wheat land as far as the eye could see. The crops were ready for harvesting and that meant more trucks and more combines, and slower going for us. That first afternoon, some folks having a picnic invited us to join them.

They were enjoying life on a state-owned-and-equipped pic-nic grounds. From then on, I kept an eye out for state-owned picnic grounds, for they proved fine places to camp as well as to eat.

The only grain available for horses in those parts was wheat grounds, but Tarzan and Rex didn't seem to mind. In fact, wheat grounds helped both of them to put on a little weight. I kept looking for oats or corn, but farmers and feed stores acted as if they'd never heard of those grains.

Uncle Waldo would have liked that country. Bird hunt-ing had been the favorite sport of his younger days, and the quail were thick along the roadsides in northwestern Kansas. Day after day, Depeche Toi ran himself silly through the thick growths of weeds. The Spaniel blood in him led him to the quail, and then the Dachshund part of him held him back from catching any. His nose was smart, but his short legs weren't speedy. It was a frustrating time for the dog. So none of us dined on quail.

Across Beaver Creek but short of St. Francis, they were almost finished building a new, four-lane section of high-way. It hadn't been opened to the public.

"You arrived three days too early," the road boss told me. "Too bad. Taking this new section of highway, you would have saved yourself over twenty miles."

"It's worse than too bad," I told him. "We're behind schedule—trying to get to Cheyenne in Wyoming for the rodeo."

"I read where they expected you. Did you say you lost the letter?"

"Letter? What letter?" I asked.

"Why, I thought you just told me that you lost the letter from the Governor of Kansas. You know, the letter giving you authority to be the first person to use this new highway. Isn't that what you just said?"

I nodded. Saying yes would have been an outright lie.

The road boss told a couple of his men to remove a bar-rier, and we walked onto the new highway. We stayed on it for the rest of that day and part of the next, and we made believe it was our own private road. There were no cars or trucks or combines. We had the four lanes to ourselves. And that night was the first time on the journey that I went to sleep in the middle of a road. I didn't mind when I rolled off the blankets while I slept. There was no spreading cactus on that cement.

So that's how we saved time getting to St. Francis and then crossing the Republican River for the second time (we'd done it before at Clay Center), and coming within a day's march of Colorado.

When we made camp that night, I figured that we could make the end of the rodeo week in Cheyenne, if we really hustled. Getting there sooner meant that we'd have to miss Denver, and I had a special reason for wanting to visit that city:

Long ago, before the first war, Mama had convinced her father to help a cousin who wanted to go West and strike it rich. Grandpa had loaned the man a hundred dollars, and staked him to a horse and buggy. The cousin had gone West and settled in Denver and made good there, but he never did make good on the loan. But his family still lived there, and I'd heard many times that they were still well off. "You get to be a millionaire by not paying your debts," was Uncle Waldo's explanation of how the Denver branch of the family had become so rich.

I just wanted to check up on the Denver branch, and see where they lived and how they were doing. I didn't intend to meet them or to try to collect the old debt. But if the Lord wanted to arrange it, I did plan on selling them some postcards. They were the Stuart side, and I was a Libby, so they wouldn't know we were related unless I told them.

Then, on that last morning in Kansas, the whole plan changed. A car carrying Wyoming license plates came along and stopped. The two men in the car were Frontier Days officials from Cheyenne, and they wanted to be sure that I'd

148

be on hand for the big opening day parade. According to them, we'd miss the whole rodeo week if we sidetripped to Denver.

"You have eight full days to make Cheyenne and be in the parade," one of them said. "You can make it if you cut across this corner of Colorado. And we're counting on you to make it! Thousands of people are waiting to see you there. We'll be happy to truck you down to Denver after the rodeo. How about it?"

So that's why we missed Denver. Instead, we started cutting across the northeast corner of Colorado. "It's a race against time, boys," I told my friends. "In our case, really a walk against time."

I'd waited a long time to see real cattle country, and now we were in it. It was worth seeing, but I would have seen more if it hadn't been so windy. Farms along the way had already done the midsummer plowing, and the winds would pick up the dry earth and blow it in our faces. Whenever it happened, Rex and Tarzan would lower their heads and I'd keep my eyes closed. Those were always northerly winds, blowing down from Wyoming. It seemed almost as though I had at least one, unknown enemy in Cheyenne.

Most days, we got an early start and stayed on the road for ten to twelve hours. It was up and down country, and I didn't dare push the horses more than that. And it was lucky that we did keep long hours, for things would happen to cause delays.

First, there was the matter of the poison. We had been invited to stay over in a stable on our second night in Colorado. Tarzan was carrying a heavy load, so I unpacked him first. He rolled on the ground when I turned to Rex, and then he walked over to a stream that was close to the stable yard.

The stableman came running and shouting, "You trying to kill that horse?" He ran to the stream, where Tarzan was

149

drinking, and pushed my horse's head out of the water. "Get him out of here!" the man yelled to me. "Some damn fool upstream put out poison for rodents."

We didn't know how much of the poisoned water Tarzan had gulped down. To be on the safe side, we called in the local vet. He gave Tarzan some medicine and told me not to worry.

"Now, don't baby him," was the vet's advice. "He should start sweating in a couple of hours, and the more he sweats the better, so keep him on the move. He won't feel well tomorrow, but travel will do him good."

I did worry, of course. I bedded down on the floor right outside his stall that night, and none of us got much sleep. Tarzan kept making funny, moaning sounds, and Rex chimed in with nickers and stomps. Then Depeche Toi started whining. Once, when I had drifted into sleep, I awakened with the dog's howling. It was a dismal night. I really expected Tarzan to die. I'd never heard a horse, or a cow, or any other animal sound so mournful. When I went to him in the stall to try and comfort him, he was wet with sweat. That was after Depeche Toi started howling.

Afterwards, I didn't get a wink of sleep. A dog howling in the night means only one thing in Maine. The only family I had was right there in the stable with me. That meaning was for one of us, and only Tarzan was sick.

If he had died, I wouldn't have gone on toward California. Rex and the dog and I would have gone on to somewhere, but not to the coast. It wouldn't have been right to continue without Tarzan.

Tarzan did pull through. I babied him to the extent of staying over a day at the stable before pushing on. He wasn't his real self as he walked through the heat of the next two days, but he sweated the poison out, just as the vet said he would. Rex carried me and most of the gear on both days.

All of us could have used more water. The culverts were dry, and I didn't have the brains to figure out how to get past the cattle gates that blocked the roads leading to houses.

They called them gates out there, although actually the gate was a bunch of separated metal strips laid across the road. A car could roll over them and a human could walk over them, but cattle and horses just wouldn't step over them for fear of catching their feet. Well, I didn't know until somebody told me that a person on horseback was supposed to open a gate in the wire fencing and get through that way. The person who told me was the nightman at a cattle sales barn where we stayed on the third night after the poisoning.

When the nightman went home, he forgot to tell me two things: I was supposed to sleep on the office couch, and that a load of cattle was expected. So I made my bed inside the barn right smack in the middle of a runway. If Depeche Toi hadn't barked when the barn doors swung open, I'd have been trampled to death by the herd of steers that had arrived. I rolled out of the way just in time.

I was beginning to think that Colorado wasn't a safe place for us, and that the sooner we got to Wyoming the better. So as soon as dawn came, I watered the horses, stowed on the gear, and settled down atop Rex. We were all set for the earliest start we had made in weeks, except that Depeche Toi had disappeared.

He was busy chasing rabbits in the pasture behind the barns. When I heard him bark, I rode around the barn, calling to him, and then I saw that he hadn't been barking at a rabbit. He was standing at attention and looking at what I thought was another dog, about fifty feet away. The stranger was brown, with pointed ears and very slim legs. He was an odd looking animal, and when he spotted me he turned tail and ran like a streak. Depeche Toi raced after him, ignoring my calls. The last I saw of the dog, he was galloping over a rise in the direction of Kansas, where we'd already been.

They told me at the barn that the strange dog wasn't a dog at all. He was a coyote, and my dog had no chance of catching him. "The dog will get the idea and come back in a few minutes," one man told me. But the minutes stretched

151

into hours, and Depeche Toi didn't return until about noon. So it was another half-day wasted, and I told my boys that we'd be lucky to get to Cheyenne by Christmas.

We camped out that night, got a proper early start the next morning and reached Greeley by nightfall. It was the only big town we saw in Colorado, and I saw more of it than I'd intended to; Rex needed new hind shoes.

As usual, we had to waste a day waiting for a blacksmith. There were still plenty of blacksmiths around, but it wasn't like the old days. You had to phone for one and then you'd wait around for him to come.

From Greeley, we pressed on north for Cheyenne. I was mixed up on my days and sure that we'd reach there a day late for the big rodeo parade.

So when we finally walked into the outskirts of Cheyenne, I was very surprised to learn that we'd arrived there on the right day.

9 ☛ WYOMING

It was the right day, but almost the wrong hour. We arrived just in time to join the riders in the parade.

There was a marching band, playing the same tune over and over: "California, Here I Come," I think. Then there were about twenty beautiful cowgirls mounted on white horses, followed by cowboys on black horses, each carrying a flag. Then I came along on Rex, with Tarzan on lead right behind us, and Depeche Toi sitting on top of him. After us there were more cowgirls on horses, and behind them were about a hundred kids who just wanted to be in a parade. Most of the kids were out of step.

There was no room for us to camp on the rodeo grounds. The place was overflowing with people. So we made camp on the shore of a nearby lake where they told me it would be all right to build a campfire on the sand. Since I did most of my own cooking in Cheyenne, the fire was a big fiscal help. Sterno heat would have been much more expensive.

Almost every night of my stay, some Boy Scouts built the fire for me. Then they'd stay around while I cooked and ate my supper, and we'd talk about all sorts of things. Some of them chipped in and bought me a fry pan. They knew all

153

about a fry pan being called a spider in Maine, but they'd never heard of the old-fashioned kind of spider my mother owned. That one had three legs and was used to set over the flame when cooking was done in the fireplace.

Every day, I'd pack the horses and ride over to the rodeo grounds and spend my time watching the events or seeing the exhibits. Hardly anyone recognized me when I was walking around, but as soon as I climbed into the saddle, everybody knew who I was and a crowd would form. I sold only a few postcards on the ground, but hundreds from the saddle. In fact, I ran out of cards in Cheyenne, and had to order more. But I didn't pick them up until I was leaving the city. I was all for making money, but it would have been greedy to sell more, and being greedy had always been against the grain with me. I didn't intend to change my character for profit.

Along about the fourth day, while I was watching the chuck-wagon races, a man started talking to me about how dangerous the races were. "I wish they'd stop having these races," he said. "The wagons often smash up, and when that happens, we can be sure the drivers suffer injuries and that one or more horses will be killed. The men know they are running a risk, but not the horses. I mean, it's not fair to the horses. You understand?"

I did, and it made me feel guilty, for I had been enjoying the races. After a few minutes, I walked away from there. The man had ruined my appetite for chuck-wagon races.

I visited a railroad transportation exhibit which included everything from stage coaches to modern engines, then went on to a show of old and new farm machinery, but I wasn't able to shake the man, or what he had said. Why, I even thought about him that night, and I supposed then that it was because he had been hatless and wearing an eastern white shirt with a regular tie. All the other men there wore hats, mostly western, and those string ties. My man had been almost as short as me, weighed less and was a little older. And he had been the only person I'd met on my

154

journey—except for Sam Hollis and her husband back in Pennsylvania—with a deep concern about animals.

During the rest of the week at the rodeo, I didn't see him again. I was too busy to go looking for him, that was for sure. My mail had caught up with me in Cheyenne, and there were a great many interesting things to see on the rodeo grounds, by night and by day: Steer riding, calf roping, wild horse racing, and all the exhibition halls. At night, I liked to stroll along the midway and listen to the barkers. They charged high prices for their shows, so I didn't get to see any. Owners of two different shows offered me jobs. The money was all right for just sitting on a platform and talking to people and selling autographs, but I'd come too far, free of strings, to get involved. Still, those offers pleased me.

My camp by the lake was on a direct line from an army air base to the rodeo grounds. Planes flew over every day, and when the pilots found out where I was located, they dipped their wings as they flew over. On the last day I was there, one pilot dropped a letter attached to a piece of iron. Fifty cents and an address for me to send one of my cards to were in the letter.

We moved out of Cheyenne on the day after the rodeo closed. Getting clear of the city took more time than planned, for people kept stopping us, and many of them had gifts of food for us. When we finally broke free, the cargo on the horses included cookies, cakes, pies, sandwiches, fried chicken, canned chicken and a loaf of banana bread, which was a new kind of bread to me. None of the food was wasted. I had learned, when young, to eat first the things that spoil quickly.

The first hills of the Laramie Range came into view twenty-four hours later. Back East, I would have said we could reach them in another day, but out there in the West I knew it would take two, or maybe three.

And three it was. There was something tricky about the

155

atmosphere in the West. When it came to distance, things always proved farther away than they looked. "It's our kind of air," folks told me out there. "Cleanest and clearest air in the world. It makes things seem closer than they really are." Maybe they were joshing me, but part of what they said was fact anyway: Things did seem closer than they really were. I'd tell the boys that a certain point up ahead was an hour away, and three hours later we'd still be short of it.

The view from the top of that first hill on the range was really spectacular. I had been atop mountains in New England and knew something about good views, but this one was a record breaker. It was a far distance yet into the town of Laramie, Wyoming, where we were heading, but we could see it all spread out to the west and below us. And we could see beyond the town to the snow-capped mountains. "Boys, take a good look at those mountains," I said. "They've already got winter on top. We can't climb over them, but we will find a mountain pass and get to the other side."

I still don't know how we got over the Laramie Range, or how the drivers of those big trucks managed those steep, curving roads. Time and again, when we heard a truck roaring downgrade behind us, I'd pull my boys off onto a dirt road. There were plenty of those little roads out into the hills, and I thought that by using them I was playing it safe. But I wasn't. What I was really doing was risking our necks.

"Stay clear of those roads," a truck driver told me one day. "Those are runaway-truck stops. Notice how you always find one at the start of a big curve? Well, when a driver loses control, he heads into one of those little roads. You'll get killed if you keep parking in them."

I thought he was pulling an Easterner's leg. So I investigated the next dirt road that we found at the start of a curve. It was level and not long, and the footing was sandy and got worse toward the end. And at the very end there was a big sand bank that would have stopped any truck that got that far.

156

After that, I was content to hug the side of the main road when those big trucks came zooming by. Getting trapped on one of those little roads would have been fatal.

The days in the Laramie Range were reasonably warm, but the nights turned unreasonably cold. I could have used my winter clothes. I still had one union suit with me. Except for the first night, I put it on every night before turning in, and darn near froze to death doing it. Watching me make the quick switch into the union probably frightened away the wild animals. Something did, that was for sure. Those big hills were supposed to be full of wild things, but I didn't even see a rabbit.

It took six days from the time I first saw Laramie until we pulled into that town, and it had been an up and down journey all the time. The road map had the mileage at sixty from Cheyenne to there, and it had taken us ten days in all to cover. We must have taken the wrong road.

I found we were as well known in Laramie as we had been in Cheyenne. A lot of the Laramie people, of course, had probably been over to the rodeo.

When I stopped to ask directions at the nearest stable, a little crowd gathered and I found myself selling postcards before I could ask the question. Then a woman asked how long I'd be staying in Laramie, and I told her I'd be there only a day or so.

"In that case, you can stay with me," she said.

She lived close by and owned several horses. It was a big house, with a shed and a fenced pasture to its rear.

After supper, she explained why she had asked how long I'd be staying in Laramie. It seemed that her husband would be home in three days. He was off somewhere on a business trip. "I just can't have anyone here when he's home. It's too embarrassing."

"Doesn't he like guests?" I asked.

"I don't know. I no longer know what he likes or what he thinks. He doesn't talk to me."

He hadn't talked to that poor woman, his own wife, in

over three years. Always before that, he had been very talkative. According to her, she hadn't done anything to cause him to stop talking. One day, right after breakfast, he had just stopped talking to her.

"I've begged him to tell me why, and he just shrugs. I've asked him to write notes, but he won't. I just haven't been able to figure it out. He talks to other people, but not to me. I blame Vermont."

That puzzled me, so I asked why.

"Because he was born there. He still loves that state, or he did up to three years ago. He hates Wyoming. Of course, everybody claims he married me for my money, although that didn't seem to bother him for the first twenty-one years of our marriage. He talked to me all that time. Yes, Vermont must be the trouble."

Many a woman I'd known would have considered a non-talking husband a blessing, but that woman in Laramie didn't. Otherwise, she had everything, including an auto agency and a store.

Well, she talked on that way about her husband until we went to bed, and I had a funny feeling that it would be best to change my plans and get out of Laramie as soon as possible. But she didn't mention her husband again, so I stayed another day there and was glad that I did.

That morning, she asked about my travel plans. I knew where I was heading, more or less: From Laramie through the mountains to Saratoga, and from there over the Continental Divide to Rock Springs, then northwest a couple of hundred miles to Boise, Idaho.

"It will be winter in the mountains in another month," she told me, "and you're not equipped for it."

At first, I didn't believe her. The very minute she said it we were standing in the middle of August. Still, she knew the country and I didn't.

"And Boise isn't the shortest route to California," she announced. "Why are you going there?"

"I promised to deliver a letter."

"Why don't you mail it?"

I explained that it was a special letter, and then didn't say any more about it. The letter was the one I was carrying from Governor Muskie of Maine to Governor Smiley of Idaho. When I had promised to deliver the letter, I had no idea it would take us so much time to get where we were. Now it looked like my escape from winter was just a temporary thing. Boise was a foolish way to get to California, but a promise was a promise.

That afternoon in Laramie, my new friend took me to her store, and there the clerks told me all the things I'd need in coming weeks. I bought as few things as possible, the main item being a sleeping bag that zipped up the side and had a hood at the top. My friend wanted to give me that and the other things, but I had money and insisted on paying for the sleeping bag. Of course, I bought it wholesale. At the regular price, I couldn't have afforded that particular sleeping bag with the zipper and hood.

Except for winter clothes, I was in pretty good shape for early winter in the mountains when we set out westward from Laramie. They'd told me all about the open range and the big mountains, but you really learn about such things by living with them, and the living wasn't easy. We climbed and climbed for days. The mid-hours ranged from warm to hot, but the nights were bitter cold. The sleeping bag was the salvation for both Depeche Toi and me. It was roomy enough, and we helped keep each other warm. I was extra careful finding places to camp, so that Rex and Tarzan could be shielded against the night winds. They had to be tired by the end of each day, but neither horse showed it. A horse just can't go on saddled and heavy loaded for hours on end and not be tired. Of course, each of them carried a hundred-pound sack of grain, and that may have inspired them to keep going until they could partake of same.

It was sheep range country for the most part. Whenever I could locate a supply camp, I was always sure of a welcome and a hot supper. The men tended sheep for a living, but they knew horses, too, and they never wasted time asking unnecessary questions. They pitched right in and helped me unload Rex and Tarzan. They fed and watered my friends before turning them loose. I never heard one of them use a bad or a dirty word. They were as gentlemanly as cattlemen when I was around.

Back in Laramie, I had been told that we could make Saratoga in three days. It took twice that time, partly because we were constantly climbing and partly because I didn't dare hurry the horses. Rex and Tarzan were sea-level horses, more or less, and now the altitude was around ten thousand feet. Both were in hard condition, but I was lung conscious because of my own condition, and feared what the high country might do to them. They didn't seem to have any trouble. I was all right when in the saddle, but if I walked for very long, I'd begin to feel dizzy. Depeche Toi was the only one who hurried. He had cast iron lungs.

We reached the snowline on the fifth day of the climb. Tarzan may have set a world's record that day. At least, I thought so and told him so: "You're the first Maine horse to stand in summertime snow in the Rockies." All four of his feet were planted in the snow when I said it.

We didn't actually travel in the snow. Our road ran along just at the edge of the snowline and led us, finally, to the campgrounds on Snowy Range Peak. We were living higher than ever before at ten thousand and eight hundred feet. And I ate higher off the hog than ever before, too. Many families were picnicking there. When they drove off for home at dusk they gave me foodstuffs that they hadn't used. Many of the things were in cans and jars. High-priced imported items that I'd read about but never tasted. My supper that night was fit for a movie queen. It was as if those people had seen right through my saddle tramp costume and knew that I was really Mesannie Hart.

From the campgrounds, it was mostly downgrade into Saratoga. We stopped at a ranch on the outskirts, went into town the next morning, and sold a few postcards. I didn't

160

have to stock up on food for myself, thanks to all the foreign items. I thought about buying another sack of grain there, but something told me to wait until we reached Rawlins, which was a three-day trek away across the North Platte River.

It was lucky that I did wait. Otherwise, I would have missed meeting one of my kin. He came into the feed store in Rawlins and said, "They told me I'd find you here. I'm Hamlin Stuart. I think we're seventh cousins."

"Fifth cousins," I told him. "I didn't know I had any kin in Wyoming."

"You didn't until last year. I moved over from Ohio. Enjoying your trip?"

"Can't complain."

"Those are nice looking horses."

We talked about this and that for another ten minutes, and then he hurried off to keep an appointment for a haircut. Except for the fact that he was overweight by about a hundred pounds, he was a typical Stuart. Unlike so many others who had told me that they admired my courage, Hamlin took it for granted that anyone with Stuart blood could and would go anywhere he set his mind to go. Maine's history would have been far different without the Stuarts. And the same can be said about the history of the whole country, according to the Stuarts.

From Rawlins, we started losing altitude. Now we had to cross the Red Desert of the Continental Divide. All I knew about deserts was what I'd learned long ago in school, so this one took me by surprise. Instead of a flat, sandy plain, it was an endless expanse of mountains and hills and rocky ridges sticking out of a bed of sand. In some places the sun had baked the sand into a white crust so hard that the horses' shoes couldn't scratch it. And where there were cracks in the sand, you could look down and see the red color beneath that gave the desert its name.

During the first few hours, I thought there was nothing around but sand and rocks and sagebrush. I didn't see how

161

anything could live in that barren country. Then I started seeing wildlife up ahead: Rabbits, rats, desert mice and a few big animals that looked like mountain goats, but weren't. They would run off and disappear before we got close. Depeche Toi had a wonderful time chasing everything and catching nothing. After the first day, he quit the chasing and stayed close, as if he knew his short legs were too much of a handicap.

The funny little rats ran so fast you could hardly see their tails. The desert was alive with them. Kangaroo rats, they called them out there, since the tails were long, shaped like a kangaroo's. They were smaller than the garbage-can variety. Sometimes I'd spot one sitting on his hind legs and tail, like a tripod, as if looking us over as we passed by, and maybe wondering what on earth we were. Some folks said the rats were good to eat. If true, there's no need to worry about anybody going hungry.

There were section-line villages all along the rail line over the desert, and we made a point of staying in them most nights. We always found salt, hay, and water in stables at those places, and often we stayed over a day or two and just plain rested. The rest was mostly needed by me. I don't know if it was the glistening of the sand or the reflected heat rays, but day's end always found my eyelids swollen and my eyes hurting. I should have worn dark glasses, but it was too late to get any by the time I needed them.

When possible, I slept inside the stables. The nights were good and cold and it was warmer inside, for one thing. Also, the snakes didn't come into the stables. "Don't worry about the snakes," I was told. "They stay away from people." I wanted to believe that when I had to camp outdoors, but I wasn't sure anybody had told the snakes they were supposed to stay away from me. So outdoors sleep was a trifle uneasy. There were more rats than snakes on the Red Desert, but that still left plenty of snakes.

We were still crossing the Red Desert when September came, going northwest and mostly west to where Utah met

162

Idaho on Wyoming's western border. We began to see more houses and gas stations and small motels, and once in a while, from a rise, I could see ranch buildings far back from the road. Then there were the "everything stores" which we called general stores back in Maine. Usually, the store seemed to be located in the middle of nowhere, and you wondered where its business came from.

I found out late one afternoon near Rock Springs when I stopped to inquire about a likely camping place. There were clouds in the sky, and I wanted to get the pup tent up and the gear covered before any rain came.

A friendly-type Spanish man owned that particular store, and he told me, "Take the next dirt road down the hill past the church. You'll find a big, dry wash with plenty of grass for the horses on the slopes."

"Church?" I asked. "Are there enough people around here to support a church?"

"You'd be surprised. The church serves a lot of territory. Not many people live along the main road, but there are quite a few ranches and small farms scattered in all directions from here. Oh, I've got plenty of neighbors. Of course, they live five or ten miles from each other, so you Easterners might not call them neighbors."

"Is there any water for my horses in that wash?"

"Not at the moment, but there will be in short order," he assured me. "From the looks of the sky, we're in for a little shower. The wash is bone dry now, but there'll be a few inches of water in the bowl of it right after the rain."

The wash was about half a mile away and just as the Spanish man had described it. Bone dry, but plenty of lush grass on the slopes. I unpacked the horses and turned them loose, then covered the gear with my poncho, fixed the tent and got the sleeping bag under it. I did it all in a hurry, and Depeche Toi and I dove into the tent just as the first drops fell out of the sky. We were on the rim of the wash, where it was flat and sandy and full of sagebrush and Russian Thistle.

163

It wasn't a heavy shower and it didn't last more than five minutes, but it served to wet the ground and provide a stream of water for Rex and Tarzan. There was a nice pool of water down in the bowl of the wash, and I hoped it wouldn't sink in too quickly so that enough would be left for drinking in the morning.

I had an early supper, then walked to the store with Depeche Toi. As I was buying a few necessary things, the Spanish man asked if I had made camp in time to keep things from getting wet.

"Just in the nick of time," I told him. "It wasn't much of a shower."

"Not here," he said, "but according to the radio, it came down real heavy in the mountains up above us. Say, I didn't notice your dog before. There's supposed to be a bitch coyote's den with a new litter somewhere near that wash. If your dog starts chasing her, she'll run him all over the state."

I promised to keep Depeche Toi close. It was almost dark when we got back to camp. I had no fear that the horses would wander during the night, for the only grass around was on the slopes of the wash. But just to be on the safe side, I hitched each of them to a Russian Thistle and gave them enough rope to reach the grass. Russian Thistle is a pest plant that takes deep root along the edges of a wash, and it is covered with nasty thorns.

In the middle of the night, I was awakened by Rex's frightened calls. At first I thought coyotes had scared him, but then, by flashlight, I found that he had tangled his rope around several of those darned thistles. He was trembling, and as I tried to quiet him Tarzan started squalling. I played my flashlight his way and saw that he wasn't tangled. Depeche Toi, who was right there with us in the wash, started barking. I couldn't figure out what was wrong.

My trouble was that I didn't have horse sense or dog sense. They knew danger was on the way, but I didn't. Then I heard a funny sound that grew into a roar. I turned just in time to get my face wet. A wall of water knocked me flat and rushed on over me. I was half drowned before I realized what had happened.

What had happened, of course, was that the runoff rain from the mountains had formed into a sudden river and ran through a long series of washes until it found ours. I couldn't swim, but I managed to scramble out of that instant flood somehow. I went most of the way on all fours, with Depeche Toi's tail in my face. Inside and out, I had never been wetter. I had swallowed gallons of water, and my clothes were soaked.

The flash flood had robbed me of the flashlight, and it had also seeped over the edge of the wash and found the gear and pup tent. The tent was down, but the sleeping bag was there. The gear was spread all over the place. Everything was soaking wet. And then I discovered the horses were gone!

They'd been scared out of their wits, yanked their halters loose, and taken off into the night.

I called out their names several times, hoping to hear answering whinnies but feared that I wouldn't, and that's the way it was. There was nothing to do except sit there in the darkness and wait. So that's what the dog and I did. After awhile, I looked up at the heavens and asked, "What did I do?" If a sign came, I missed it.

Depeche Toi and I waited for the horses, but the only thing that came along, hours later, was the dawn.

When it was light enough to see, I collected our belongings and hung the lighter things over the sagebrush. The soggy blankets were too heavy for the sage, so I strung rope between big thistles and hung the blankets that way. The big thistles had held fast when the horses yanked themselves free, so I knew they were strong enough to support the blankets, the sleeping bags, and other things. Then I told Depeche Toi to stay there and guard things while I went looking for the horses.

I found fresh tracks near the church, but nowhere else.

165

Then I walked to the store and waited there for the Spanish man to arrive and open up for the day. I didn't have to wait very long. He was an early opener.

"I don't understand how you got caught like that," he said. "Didn't you hear me when I said they'd had heavy rains in the mountains? Why, any darn fool knows that a wash is no place to stay near when that happens. I thought sure that you'd have the brains to move camp up higher near the church. Don't you Easterners ever use your heads? I can't understand how you got this far, knowing as little as you do about simple things like flash floods!"

He scolded me for about ten minutes, interrupting the lecture just twice: Once to phone the sheriff about the horses, and the other time to phone his wife and tell her to come to my rescue.

The sheriff from Rock Springs got there first. I had to tell him the whole sorrowful tale of the night before, and he kept laughing fit to bust. It was a tragic retelling for me, for I'd lost my horses, nearly drowned, and everything I owned was a soggy mess. The store owner was too polite to laugh, but he had to smile now and again.

"Funniest story I ever heard," the sheriff told me. "Now don't you worry about the horses. By this time, somebody has found them. I'll run back to the office and get the word around. You stay right here."

After the sheriff left, the Spanish man said, "He's right. If the horses didn't head into the mountains, somebody has found them by now."

I didn't say anything. If I knew Rex, and I did, he was heading back for Tennessee and Tarzan was tagging along behind him. Remembering what had happened in the big swamp in Arkansas, I figured my boys were down the road that we'd come up the day before.

The storeman's wife couldn't have been more helpful. She was the handsomest woman I'd ever seen. She drove me to their house and prepared a hot breakfast for me. Then she offered me a choice of old clothes to wear until my own

166

things became dry. While there, I talked to the sheriff on the phone.

"No word yet," he reported. "But as I said before, don't worry. Somebody has found them by now, and most folks around here are honest. Of course, some do steal loose horses that aren't branded, but people like that sleep late." He laughed at his own joke when he hung up the phone.

The mention of horse thieves was on my mind when we drove back to the store. "Do people around here still steal horses?" I asked.

"It does happen," the storeman's wife told me, "but nobody would be fool enough to risk stealing yours. I wouldn't be surprised if they are the best known horses in America by now."

Within the hour, both of us were proven right. She was right, because the man who found Rex and Tarzan notified the sheriff. I was right, because he found them almost thirty miles down the road where we'd been two days before.

The state police drove me and the dog back to the horses. I took along just one saddle, leaving the other one and all the wet gear with the storeman's wife, who promised to get everything dry.

So by early afternoon, I was in the saddle atop Rex again and my little caravan started covering the identical miles we had covered two days before. For the two nights on the way back to Rock Springs, the state police had arranged for us to stay with a family the first night and at a motel on the second. So I didn't worry about flash floods anymore on that trip.

The whole affair sort of shook my belief in foreordainment. Why had the flood picked on me? Why hadn't anyone else in Wyoming lost his horses? If Somebody was making such things happen, what had I done to deserve them?

Was it possible that I wasn't supposed to reach California? I kept asking myself that. Maybe I could have found the answer by tossing another coin, but I lacked the courage to try it right then.

Now it was Tarzan's turn for new hind shoes. That meant a three-day layover in Rock Springs while we waited for the blacksmith to come back from some work he was doing in the hills. About half of my stock of postcards had been ruined by the wetness, so I had a new batch printed up. Otherwise, I rested and so did the boys. The Red Desert and the extra trip left all of us a touch weary.

The smithy who shoed Tarzan was the least cheerful member of his trade whom we'd met on the whole journey. "You'll never make California with these horses," he told me.

"Why, what's wrong with my horses?"

"It ain't the horses so much as the winter. The snows come early out in these parts. You'd be smart to hole up some place and wait for spring."

He was shocked when I told him that I was toying with the idea of visiting Yellowstone National Park before swinging over to Idaho. It didn't mean anything to him that I'd wanted to see the park since I was a little girl.

"Are you out of your mind?" he asked. "Why, Yellowstone is full of bears! And bears favor horses in their diet, and they eat anything they can find just before they go into hibernation."

He refused to accept payment for the shoes. "I'm a religious man," he assured me. "What would the Lord think if I made a profit out of fixing this horse to carry you to your doom?"

We saw him again the next morning as we pulled out for Green River. He was standing on a corner, watching us. When I waved, he tipped his hat. His face was glum and he didn't smile. I'd hoped that he wasn't a prophet.

I was glum on the next morning. We had stayed the night at a ranch where they had a wild horse in the corral next to Tarzan and Rex. Some men had captured him three weeks before, after cutting him from a herd and driving him into a blind canyon. Some said his dam was a Morgan mare; but no matter his blood, that was the handsomest horse I'd ever seen. A chestnut of about fifteen hands. He was friendly over the fence with my boys, but you could see that fright was still in his eyes. I fell in love with him and they offered him to me cheap. I would have had to work him between my boys, and three horses abreast took up too much space on the roads. When we left that Green River ranch, the wild fellow nickered after us.

The town of Green River was on the banks of Green River. We passed through one and crossed the other, then headed on through flat lands for several days. You could look up ahead on the main road and see an endless string of telephone poles, but very little else. Houses, when we saw any, were clustered around railway yards. The people depended on tank cars for most of their water.

It was lucky that we were carrying plenty of grain. Bunch grass grew through there, but you had to know where to find it, and there wasn't much of it along the main road. There was a sameness to that country, and day after day I'd keep thinking we'd passed by the same points and seen the same scenery the day before. The nights were all the same, too. When dusk came, the winds would blow and whistle all through the black hours. When they let up, you could bet dawn wasn't far away. I got a little tired of it all after about a week. It seemed like it would never end.

That was the main reason why we took a side trip into the mountains. I knew there'd be better grass up there, and maybe some ranches where we could find shelter and water. Of course, it was high time the horses had some relief from hard pavements and traffic, too. We were in no danger of getting lost. In those parts, all side roads led to the main road sooner or later.

We were put up at small ranches the first two nights. The hay spoiled Tarzan and Rex. After those stays, they wouldn't look at bunch grass.

Along about noon on our third day in the mountains, our road came to a fork. I was up on Rex, and it didn't make any difference to me which branch we took. I let the horse make up his own mind. Rex proved his smartness.

169

He decided on the right-hand branch, the one that ran downgrade.

An hour later, just after we'd rounded a curve, I pulled him up short. A hundred yards ahead was a little farmhouse. It looked white and fresh painted, but otherwise it seemed the carbon copy of the little house we'd left back in Maine. And the old barn to the rear looked about the size of my old one, although in much better condition. We were standing in western Wyoming, but the place looked like it had just been flown in from New England. It did lack a picket fence, but so did my place in Minot.

Depeche Toi trotted up ahead and disappeared into the yard. I told Tarzan to move on, and as we walked along, I could almost see Uncle Waldo opening the front door and stepping out.

The door did open. I recognized the man who stepped out as the one who had complained at the rodeo in Cheyenne. The one who had said that those chuck-wagon races were too dangerous for horses.

"Why, hello," he said. "Remember me? Cheyenne in July?"

"I do," I said, but he may not have heard me. Depeche Toi was jumping up on his leg, and he was petting the dog as if they were old friends.

Then he looked up at me and said, "Let's bring your horses out back. You're just in time for lunch."

"Shouldn't you ask your wife?"

"My wife would be pleased to have you, too, except that I don't have a wife."

He said it the way an Augusta, Maine lawyer would have said it. Dry and matter of fact. Then he took Rex's lead rope from me and led us around to the barnyard.

"If you're not in a hurry, we might as well unpack," he said. He was already taking the gear off Rex, so I started on Tarzan. "Strip them down, saddle and all. There's a fine stand of grass behind the barn and a pool of water."

"I'd better hitch them. I don't trust this Rex anymore."

170

"Don't bother. They won't stray. Adam and Eve will see to that."

Then he turned to the house and whistled. Two old dogs came jumping out of an open window and trotted to him. "Keep an eye on these horses," he told them. Adam and Eve were Border Collies. They crouched and watched the horses, but paid no attention to Depeche Toi. "Those two are the best herders I ever owned. In their younger days, they could handle up to five hundred goats."

The man's name was Harvey Kelsey, and he was a goat rancher. On that day, his two men were out in the hills with close to a hundred goats, and he didn't expect them back for another month.

"It gets a little lonely here at times," he said, as we walked to his house. "You're the first traveler to come by here in a week."

The inside of the house was neat as a pin. Harvey was a better housekeeper than I had ever been. The kitchen was in the same corner as mine back in Maine, but instead of a dining room and parlor, he had just one big room.

While I washed, he busied himself setting the table. When I offered to help in the kitchen, he told me everything was about ready and to make myself comfortable at the table.

I considered it a pretty fancy table for a goat rancher. Wax flowers for a center piece, two ivory candles in glass holders, and a clean Irish linen tablecloth, plus linen napkins to match. It was daytime, so the candles weren't lit.

Lunch was a beef stew with tomatoes, carrots, potatoes, onions and other vegetables, and plenty of beef. Harvey was a good cook, and quite a baker, too. I must have eaten half a loaf of his homemade black rye. We also had goat cheese and giant ripe pears. Afterwards, we had coffee while Depeche Toi gobbled down some stew that had been cooling in a dish for him.

"I was eighty in December," Harvey told me. "I'd judge you to be somewhere in your early fifties."

171

"Sixty-three in December," I admitted. He was older than I had thought.

"You look much younger. Must be the outdoor life. What day in December?"

Well, it turned out that we shared the same birthdate—December 13th! Another coincidence was that horses had brought him to Wyoming, too. In his case, the horses had pulled a wagon, and he and his parents rode in the wagon all the way from Pennsylvania. That was back in 1890, the year Wyoming became a state. "We got started out here at the same time, the state and I," was the way he put it.

When he invited me to stay there a few days, he was also quick to explain that he'd sleep in the barn. I told him I'd dallied enough the last few days and had to push on for Boise. "And after that," I explained, "I'll make a bee line for California. I'm the last of my line, but I'll be the first of my line to see California."

"I'm the last of my line, too, and I'll probably never see California. Why is seeing California so important to you?"

"For one thing, I promised myself."

Harvey just looked at me, as if waiting for me to say more, but I didn't know what else to say. Also, I had a funny feeling that he had something special to say, but didn't know quite how to say it.

Finally, he smiled and said, "I asked for a personal reason. Now I don't know what your beliefs are, but I'll tell you one of mine: I believe that all things are foreordained by some Higher Power. Nothing really happens by chance, you see. Why were you and I born on the same day of the month? Why did we both come to Wyoming? Why did we meet as strangers in Cheyenne? Why did you select this road to travel?"

"Rex chose it," I explained.

"You see? Even his action was foreordained. And all these things happen for a purpose. Now then, I don't mean to startle you, but I'm hoping that you will remain here as my wife."

I came close to spilling my coffee and had to put the cup down. I wasn't even sure that I'd heard right. "Are you proposing?" I asked.

He nodded, and I stared at him.

"You don't know anything about me," I said.

"I know a great deal about you. I've been reading about you for months. And I know too that you love animals. What will happen to my goats when I'm gone? What will happen to my ranch?"

"But you've known me for less than two hours."

"That's true," he agreed. "But how do you know that I haven't been waiting for these two hours since 1890?"

Well, the man was serious, all right. Or serious enough to offer to put half the ranch in my name then and there, and will me the other half in case he went to his reward first. I told him that I never had rushed into things and that I would have to think about his offer.

"I understand," he said. "My proposal will last as long as I do. It isn't likely that I'll meet another woman like you."

Then he asked if I needed any money for my journey. I told him that I had plenty. The plenty amounted to about three dollars just then, but I didn't mention the sum to him.

When we took to the road again that afternoon, he remarked: "I'll be waiting. Come back as soon as you can. But if your decision is no, please don't write. So long as I don't know you won't return, I can keep on hoping."

I managed to nod, and then we moved on down the road. I looked back just once and waved. I was feeling giddy, and happy and unhappy, all at the same time.

We started looking for the main road. Harvey had said it was about ten miles away, but darkness came before we got that far. Then, far up ahead, we saw the headlights of racing cars.

It was downgrade all the way, and when we got closer I saw that there was a little river between us and the main road. There was no bridge, so I looked for a shallow place to ford. I was up on Rex, and I moved him along the bank until we came to a place where the moonlight reflected on the water in such a way that I was sure we'd found the right spot. I brought Tarzan in close and we moved ahead. Then Rex snorted and backed off. I climbed off to investigate, and held onto the end of his reins as I stepped ahead to the edge of the bank. The next thing I knew, I was dangling about ten feet above the river; the bank had caved in. The river had undercut the bank at that very point, and the moonlight's reflection had deceived me!

I yelled at Rex. He was holding his head low, giving me the full length of the reins, but if I fell more, my weight might tear his bit and headstall. I wanted his head up, but Rex didn't understand. Then Depeche Toi started barking and jumped right under Rex's nose. The horse's head went up and he backed off, pulling me with him.

So, I decided against fording the river before daylight. We camped well back from the bank, and I had a hard time getting to sleep that night. Had it been foreordained for me to drown in Wyoming? What with the flash flood at Rock Springs and the cave-in there at the river called Muddy Creek, it sure seemed that way.

Right then and there, I determined to get out of Wyoming as fast as the boys could travel.

We went through cattle country all the rest of the way to the border. It was like earlier times in the East again with people inviting us to stay with them almost every night. So it was one ranch after the other until we got into the state's western section.

One night, we made camp two hoots and a hello from Utah. We were that close.

The next night, Depeche Toi and I slept on the ground in Wyoming, while Tarzan and Rex, hitched a hundred feet away, grazed in Idaho.

10 ☛ IDAHO—OREGON

I had escaped drowning in Wyoming, but more water troubles were directly ahead in Idaho. We trudged on through heavy, cold rain for more than a week. The motels out that way had corrals, and we could always find a stable, so there was no need to camp out. But the daylight hours were too wet for comfort, and one day we covered less than five miles. It took us ten days to make up the eighty miles into Soda Springs, Idaho. Then we held up at a stable near there for a couple of days so that the horses could get new shoes all around, with rubber pads up front. The new shoes were gifts from a Lions Club. I was low on cash and couldn't pay for them myself. I could remember when a new set of shoes all around cost a dollar, or twenty-five cents more in winter when calks had to be sharp, but those days had gone forever.

After the weather cleared, we started on again. Beyond Soda Springs, we turned off the main road and followed a dirt secondary that ran along the Portneuf River up into the Portneuf Range. It was the original trail of Lewis and Clark, the one the ox-teams took later on—the oldest road into the northwest. "This is a sentimental sidetrip, boys,"

I told my friends. "One of my ancestors was with Lewis and Clark." His name was either John Libby or Jonathan Libby. Mama had his name written in her old family Bible, long since lost.

We found the ford where Lewis and Clark had crossed the river. They had piled boulders to make a way down the steep bank, but only the biggest ones were still there. Souvenir hunters had taken the smaller boulders. I was told that many relics were still buried in the mud of the river. Bones and old utensils washed up on the bank now and again, but nothing showed while I was there.

From the ford, the Lewis and Clark road wound up through a mountain pass and then joined the main road. It was about a mile to a little town where a gas station man asked, "Looking for a stable?"

"No. I'm more interested in open country and a likely place to camp tonight. Looks like we're in for a spell of fair weather."

"You carrying a gun?"

"No. My dog's all the protection I need."

"I'll tell you something, lady: You need a gun in Idaho's mountains. Wolf, lynx, cougar and bear. Last week, they shot a grizzly that weighed over five hundred pounds. He was after some kid's pony. Happened a couple of miles from here. So if you plan on camping out, you just better get yourself a gun."

I figured he was trying to put the scare into this old saddle tramp from Maine, but I thanked him for the advice anyway. But at the feed store, where we stocked up on grain, they told me much the same thing.

"You'd best find safe shelter at night," the feed man told me. "Of course, the horses would be in more danger from wild animals than you."

"Yes," said another fellow, "your main danger will be in freezing to death. Real winter is just around the corner. And a gun won't help much, unless you intend to stay awake all night long. A bear strikes quickly for a big animal."

176

"Where's the nearest stable?" I asked. "Looks like a storm in the sky."

I was sure He was still looking out for me, but did wolves and bears listen to Him?

We journeyed on to Pocatello, where I hoped to pick up some mail. It was Idaho's second largest town at the time—twenty-five thousand people or so—and the road into it went down a steep pitch, around a curve and through a narrow tunnel.

It was growing dusk when we started down the pitch. Traffic was heavy in both directions, and I had my hands full trying to keep the horses down to a walk. They knew the end of their working day was near, but I knew that most of their flank girths were loose and that any jarring would roll their loads onto the road.

Car horns sounded behind us, but there was no shoulder or other place to step aside. All we could do was walk slowly ahead and through the tunnel and up the grade on the other side. Finally, where the road widened a bit, a police officer waved us to one side.

"Look behind you," he laughed. "You have over three miles of traffic piled up. Even the cross streets are clogged. You are responsible for the biggest traffic jam in the history of Pocatello."

When I asked for directions to the post office, he started giving them to me, and then stopped and shook his head. "No," he said, "you'd just tie up more traffic, and this is our busiest hour. Let's get your livestock into the parking lot over there. I'll keep an eye on them while you walk to the post office. It's only a few blocks."

I put Depeche Toi atop Tarzan, so that he'd be out of the way of cars leaving the lot. Then I handed both reins to the officer, but forgot to tell him not to let go of Rex's bridle. That Tennessee horse didn't always take to strangers.

The post office was still open, but I couldn't claim my

mail. "Yes, we do have mail for you," a clerk told me, "but it's been here over ten days and only the head postmaster can release it, and he's gone home. Your mail is filed under 'Horse Traveler—Hold Indefinite Period.' Sorry. Come back tomorrow."

So after all the trouble, I went back to the parking lot without my mail. I wondered what the crowd was doing there, and then I saw for myself: My boys were putting on a circus act. Rex was in the middle of the lot, holding his head high and backing in tight circles. And he was snorting in fine style. Trotting around him in big circles was Tarzan. He had his ears flat and he was snorting, too. Tarzan was telling six policemen to keep their distance, and so was Depeche Toi, who was still on top of him. The dog and the horse acted as if Rex was in mortal danger and needed their protection.

Tarzan nickered and stopped clowning when he saw me. The circus act was over and the crowd drifted away.

"As soon as you were gone, the big horse yanked free," the first policeman told me. "I ran for him, and then Tarzan started chasing me. I don't think they have any respect for the law. Where's your mail?"

I explained, and said that I would have to return in the morning.

"Spare us, please," he said. "I'll pick it up and bring it to you. Where are you staying?"

I gave him the name of my stable, and he promised to bring my mail there early the next morning. So we were already packed and waiting the next morning when he phoned to say that the stable was outside the town limits and he couldn't bring it to me. "Call the sheriff," he said.

Well, the stableman was a good friend of the sheriff's deputy. He called the deputy and then told me, "Fred will have your mail here by ten-thirty."

I kept the horses packed all day waiting for Fred. He showed up with my mail just before ten-thirty on the next day. We were packed again and waiting for him, and wasted no time finding the road that would eventually lead us to Boise. The new mail that we carried ran to over hundreds of letters and cards.

I read most of them during the next two days on the walk to American Falls. There was a fine, state campground there, and from the numbers of people already camped, I judged they had the bears and wolves under control. Register Camp was the name of the place, although many still called it Massacre Camp, for that was where the wagon train survivors of an Indian ambush had buried their dead. If I'd heard that in the first place, I might not have stopped there.

The state made all campers sign the register, so I wrote down my name and other information. For make of car I wrote "Lord's Own," and for horsepower I wrote "Two." Nobody said anything to me about it. Maybe nobody ever read the register.

I pitched the pup tent near a brook where there was plenty of green grass for the boys, and I was just about to get the heater going for supper when folks started arriving from their trailers and tents. They had joined hands to fix a hot supper for me, and had a plate of meat scraps for Depeche Toi. They stayed around for an hour or so, chatting, and later some of the men sang a song about the eyes of Texas being upon me. All were from out-of-state, and not a one knew an Idaho song. The party broke up about ten that night.

I had checked the horses and just climbed into my sleeping bag when one of the women came back with a pot of hot coffee. She wanted to talk, so I climbed out of my sleeping bag and joined her.

"I didn't want to say anything in front of the others," she started. "Now just why have you been gadding around the country dressed like a man?"

"For comfort, mostly."

179

"Well, I think what you're doing is most unladylike. I know these are modern times, but a woman your age should stay at home. Why, people all over the country are laughing at you." She paused, then asked, "Do you mind? My saying such things to you, I mean?"

"Not at all," I said. And then, since she was no spring chicken, I asked, "And why don't you stay at home?"

"I'm always at home. My husband and I live in the trailer. And I wouldn't be caught dead dressed like a man. Oh, do you have an extra postcard?"

She bought three. I figured she was a woman of high morals, and my opinion only lasted until late the next morning when the state police dropped by and arrested her and the husband. They were wanted for thievery, and the man was not her husband. I heard they had even stolen the trailer.

The card business boomed that day. It was the first place in Idaho where I sold more than five or six, and the new money put my mind at ease. I really needed warmer clothes and you couldn't predict when the horses would need new shoes, mostly the hind ones.

We stayed one more night at the state camp, then got an early morning start on a fifty-mile sidetrip through the Snake River Basin to a park called "Craters of the Moon." Our reward for three days of travel was the chance to look down into the caved-in centers of long dead volcanoes. We were a few million years late to really see anything interesting.

Now it was October. I swore off taking any more side trips. We had to reach Boise and deliver that letter to the governor. After that, I figured we'd go directly as possible toward California. I knew that the Lord couldn't hold back winter just for me, and that somewhere along the line the snows would stop us. Wherever that happened, I'd have to find a job and hibernate until spring. I was sure somebody would give me a job. Work is one thing that is foreordained for average people, and there was nothing unusual about me.

It was an easy road to follow, with mountains on one side and ravines on the other. But the towns were thirty and forty miles apart, and finding water between them was our one real problem. For the most part, we solved this problem at gas stations, where the water came from wells or was piped from the river. There weren't many houses along that road.

We wandered along through towns named Twin Falls, Buhl, Thousand Springs, Hagerman, and Mountain Home. That brought us well into October and two days' distance from Boise.

I was watering the horses at a gas station when a car pulled in and stopped. "I'm a deputy sheriff from Boise," the driver said. "We heard you were this side of Mountain Home. When do you plan on reaching Boise?"

"Late tomorrow, if things go well."

"We have rooms for you at the best hotel in town. How does that sound to you?"

"Why a hotel?" I asked. "Don't you have heat in the jail?"

"If that's the way you want it, so be it," he said. "Do you know where you're staying tonight?"

"No. I'll start worrying about that in another hour or so."

"I'll see if I can arrange something," he promised. Then he drove off toward Boise, and we started down the same road.

An hour later, he returned with the news that we were expected at an inn called The Old Stage Stop. It was off the main road, so he told me just how to get there. "It will be dark soon, so I left some markers at the turns for you. Turn left when you see a row of beer cans. Go about a mile and turn right when you see a pile of old autochrome in the road. Then go straight to where there are three branches and take the one marked by more beer cans. The inn is a half mile from there."

If that deputy was the Lord's messenger, he was the first one to use beer cans to show us the way. We found the inn without trouble, and all of us rested in high style that night. Despite the late hour of our arrival, they gave me a good supper. While I enjoyed it, Tarzan and Rex chomped alfalfa inside the first stone stable any of us had ever seen. Depeche Toi decided to spend the night in the kitchen, playing with some cats.

The next afternoon a group of horsemen rode out to meet us as we came into the outskirts of Boise. They were members of a group called The Passetts, and every one was mounted on a beautiful horse. The horses had been scrubbed until they shined, and the silver trimmings on their leather had been polished so that it sparkled. There must have been thirty of those costumed Passetts, and they escorted us all the way to the jail. People along the streets waved as we passed by, and others leaned out the windows of buildings and waved. I felt like a general.

Depeche Toi and I were the only occupants of a long room that had two rows of beds. We weren't locked in, but a night guard kept circling the room, and the dog kept barking at him. I didn't get much sleep.

Next day, I had a tasty lunch with the jail officers and the guards. It was exactly the same food served to the prisoners, except we had a special cake that had been baked in my honor. Depeche Toi was present and they served him, too.

In the afternoon, I walked to the State House with the letter for Governor Smiley in my hand. Dressed as I was, I had some doubt that they would let me enter his office, but nobody stopped me. I walked right past his door several times before I had the courage to open it and walk through.

A well dressed young man stepped up to me and asked, "Yes? May I help you?"

He didn't look old enough to be a governor, so I said, "I'm looking for Governor Smiley. I have this letter for him."

"Thank you very much. I'll see that he gets it."

182

He put out his hand, but I held onto the letter. "Governor Muskie of Maine wants me to deliver this letter in person," I told him.

He smiled and said, "The governor is a very busy man. I'm afraid his schedule is filled for today. I suggest you mail the letter." Then he opened the door for me and I walked out. If my face wasn't red, it had every right to be. I was mad as a hornet! There I'd come hundreds of miles out of my way with that darned letter, and now I wasn't able to deliver it. It was an insult to Maine, and I intended to tell it to the next reporter I talked to!

A couple of minutes later, while I was still in the State House and trying to find my way out, the same young man came running after me. He grabbed my arm and said, "Governor Smiley wants to see you right now. I'm sorry I didn't recognize you."

"Don't apologize," I told him. "Nobody knows me when I'm out of the saddle."

Governor Smiley proved to be a friendly sort. He shook hands with me and took me into his private office. I gave him the letter from Governor Muskie, and he read it right away. He didn't say what was in the letter, and I didn't ask him. While he was reading, I was looking at a giant-sized potato that was on a nearby table.

The Governor caught me looking at it and said, "That's an Idaho potato. Biggest one ever grown. We think it's a world record."

It was a real big one, that's for sure. The size of a Maine melon, but more oval and flat. The skin was smooth and reddish. "It has the color of the old type Carmen," I said. "The Carmen was popular in Maine about fifty years ago."

"I want you to have this one," he said. "I thought of having it preserved for one of our museums, but when I heard you were coming this way, I thought it would make a nice gift from Idaho to you. Something to make you remember us."

"Thank you, but it wouldn't be right to take it away from

its home state," I said. "But I'd say you were wrong about it being a world's record potato. I've seen bigger ones at Maine fairs. Usually a Green Mountain." I was kidding, of course. This beautiful Idaho potato was too big to be true. I was aching to touch it, but didn't know how to go about it. It looked real, but I thought it was plastic or shaped from clay.

We chatted for about twenty minutes about potatoes, prices, duty-free farm products exchanged with Canada, and related subjects. Governor Smiley didn't strike me as the political type, but I could see why people voted for him. He reminded me of the only doctor Uncle Waldo had ever trusted.

I walked back to the jail, and a guard told me to go to the office for a telephone call. Somebody had been trying to reach me long distance. It took about five minutes for the operators to get the lines cleared, and then I was talking to a Mr. Fox in California.

"I'm with the Art Linkletter show," he told me. "When you get to Los Angeles, Mr. Linkletter would like you to be on his show. How about it?"

"Suits me," I said. "The only trouble is, I may not get to Los Angeles."

"Why not?"

"I'm not getting any younger, and at this rate it might take me years to get there."

"We're all sure that you'll make it. Mr. Linkletter wants you to know that you can count on him for help at any time. Do you have a pencil? I'll give you our phone number."

When I hung up the phone, the deputy who had let me use his desk said, "Lucky you. You're well known now, but after the Art Linkletter show, even people who can't read will know about you. You'll be famous!"

That sounded fine. "Who is this Linkletter?" I asked.

"Are you kidding? You don't know Linkletter?"

"It's not a Maine family. Not an old Maine family, anyway."

"The biggest name in radio and television, that's who Art Linkletter is! Don't you ever listen to the radio? Don't you ever watch television?"

I laughed and got out of there fast. I could have told that deputy a lot of things about me that he wouldn't have believed. I was sixty-three, almost sixty-four, and I had yet to see a talking movie. I had owned a radio since before the war. But we listened mostly to early morning weather reports. There was never much time to listen for pleasure, and when I had the time, I couldn't sit still for long. But Mama had a favorite radio program. She liked to hear Rudy Vallee. He was the only big radio star I could recall. One time, when he got married, Mama wouldn't believe it. "He's too good for any woman," she'd said.

As for television, I'd never owned a set, and I don't suppose I'd seen twenty shows in my life, and most of them had been in homes on this trip.

You're never too old to learn. That afternoon in Boise, I learned about Art Linkletter.

Next morning, I picked up my mail at the Boise post office. The bundle amounted to less than fifty letters, which surprised me. I figured people were getting tired of reading about me; but eight letters contained one-dollar bills and another one carried a five-dollar bill. Thirteen had always been my lucky number. I wrote immediate thank-you notes, and then bought two warm, wool shirts and a pair of drill jeans. After that, I rode Rex around town and sold a few postcards.

I had already grained the horses the next morning and was about to saddle and stow the gear when word came that the governor wanted to see me at the State House. I finished what I had started, and then the four of us went over to the State House. We were all set to take to the road again, and I hoped that we wouldn't have to carry that big Idaho potato.

185

Well, a television network was shooting a film for a program about Boise. Governor Smiley, the chief of police, and some other important people were waiting for us on the capitol steps, and three cameras were ready to start shooting. I hitched Tarzan and Rex to parking meters and joined them.

Sure enough, the governor offered me that big potato. And once again, I thanked him and refused it. I couldn't believe it, but it was an honest-to-goodness potato!

Then the chief of police stepped up and presented me with a permit that allowed me to hitch the horses anywhere and anytime in Boise. He also gave me a gold key for Depeche Toi. It was supposed to get him into any doghouse in town.

Next, a member of the Passetts gave me a souvenir of the Lewis and Clark expedition: A short axe handle.

When I returned to the horses, a motorcycle officer started to make out a ticket. "It's against the law to hitch a horse to a parking meter," he told me. I showed him my new permit and he tore up the ticket. I didn't think the permit was legal, but Governor Smiley was standing right there, and the officer was a smart one.

The governor helped me mount Rex. Then he had to rush off to catch a plane for somewhere, and the boys and I went looking for the main road to Caldwell, Payette and the Oregon line.

The deputies at the Boise jail had told me that we would reach Oregon in three days, or four at the most. The weather was fair, but bitter cold. I dressed as warm as possible with the new jeans over the old ones, and both new wool shirts over a cotton one.

But the three or four days stretched out into almost three weeks. We were going through Mormon country, and those people went out of their way to be nice to us. They took the dog and me into their homes and fed us, and they saw to it that the horses were sheltered and fed.

The Mormon folks were divided into those of that name

and others called Jack Mormons. A Jack Mormon was one who smoked or drank coffee. (I never met one who drank liquor.) In a family of Mormons, there might be a Jack Mormon. We stayed with a woman and her brother one night. She drank coffee and was a Jack Mormon. He didn't drink or smoke so he was just a regular Mormon.

I was running a bad cold when we left Boise, and it got worse, so that was what held us up and not the weather. The cold made my usual coughing sound like a bark, and I felt miserable all over. We stayed at different homes, none of them too far apart, for periods of several days. When I figured we'd stayed long enough, we moved on.

We were within sight of the Snake River and Oregon when a lady took pity on us and brought us to a small hotel owned by her husband. We were there for nine days, or until my cold broke.

We walked through Ontario, Oregon and put the town at our backs just one year after three of the four of us had left Minot, Maine. It was our second November 7 on the road.

The countryside looked much the same as in Maine, with rows of rocks between the fields and farmhouses built where bluffs could protect them against the north and west winds. The houses would have fit right into Maine, the chief difference being that in Oregon they didn't sit over their own cellars. The cellars out there were made of stones and covered with earth and built away from the house, like the old-time root cellars back in the East.

The road led us into mountain country again where you could travel on for hours without seeing a house. I made it a habit to accept an invitation at any hour in the afternoon. It wasn't that I was afraid to sleep on the ground, but I was thinking again about wolves and bears.

Most of the families we stayed with were Mormons, and a few were on the lookout for us, having heard from friends

over the line in Idaho. They were always kind and thought-
ful, and even the children had a way with horses. Not many
of them owned cats, so Depeche Toi didn't play too much
along that stretch.

We got beyond Juntura and headed down into the
Drewsey Valley where there was one sandy hill after the
other. A woman stopped her car and asked where we'd be
staying that night, and I told her, "No particular place,
but it will be closer to California than here." We were heading south for a change, and far to the south was California.

The woman bought a postcard and then drove off in her
car, but two hours later she was back again. "Come, get off
your horse and sit on a rock," she said. "You won't get to
California unless you can see the way."

She owned a beauty parlor and she'd brought her tools
with her. My hair hadn't been cut for months and was falling in front of my eyes, when I didn't tuck it up. She gave
me a medium cut and trimmed it on the side like a boy's.
When she was done, she stepped back and studied me for
a bit before saying, "Don't be surprised if people mistake
you for Mary Martin."

The puzzlement must have showed in my eyes. I thought
she had said "Mary Morton" with a western accent, but she
explained that she had meant a certain stage star. The Mary
Morton of Kennebunk had never been my look-alike. Long
since dead, anyway. Well, I hid my ignorance by saying
something like, "Oh, yes, that Mary. She's a friend of Bert
Linkletter."

Before leaving, the beauty-parlor woman told me she'd
fixed it for me to stay with a customer friend of hers down
the road about four miles. The friend was a wife of a
rancher named Edward Thienes and their place was about
a half mile off the main road.

They were just getting started in cattle. Mrs. Thienes
greeted me and gave me a whole bunkhouse to myself.
"You'll find it very comfortable," she said, and that was
the truth. The place even had a stove, although I didn't get

to use it. She brought me a very nice, hot supper and apologized that her husband wasn't there to meet me. She expected him back late that night. "We lived here while we were building the main house, so I know you'll keep warm," she said. "But if you do get too cold, please light the stove."

Mr. Thienes was the first person I met the next morning. He knocked on the door and invited me to join the family for breakfast at the house. "And I'm sorry about last night," he said. "My wife should have invited you to stay in the house. But she's from Boston, and has only lived out here for three years. She doesn't fully understand the Code of the West, I suppose."

"There was nothing wrong with her Boston code," I told him. "I had a good night's sleep."

After breakfast, I went looking for my horses. Mrs. Thienes had told me to put them in the pasture with some cattle the night before. I'd opened the gate in the fence line for them and then closed it, and when last seen they had been munching some lush, green grass close to some cows.

Now, in the morning, I noticed that the fencing didn't run very far, and the horses and the cattle weren't in sight. What the woman had called a pasture was more like open range. I called out Tarzan's name, but the wind was blowing my way. Then it started to rain.

"Don't worry, they won't get lost," Mr. Thienes assured me. "They're down in the valley somewhere where it's more sheltered. When this rain lets up, they'll follow my horses in for grain and we'll shut them in the yard tonight. Hope this rain doesn't turn to snow."

I wasn't worried about snow just then. Rex was on my mind. That fool was almost certain to head back for Tennessee.

But I was wrong. Close to dusk, a group of horses arrived and Rex and Tarzan were with them. They stayed safe in the yard that night, and I didn't have to go looking for them in the morning. The rain was gone by then, but not

189

the cold wind. When Mr. Thienes came out to help me pack my gear, he said there had been heavy snow in the mountains during the night. I had heard better news. Our road ran right into the mountains.

It wasn't so bad through the valley. The hills sheltered us from the wind, and in places I felt almost warm. But it turned more than chilly and the wind was razor sharp from the north when we started climbing the mountains. We were heading up to a mile above sea level and into real winter. The town of Burns was another day away, and when we got there, I planned to see what I could do about buying some winter clothes. The parka was my only coat, and my heavy gloves were ripped in the thumbs.

We looked for a certain stable—the only stable really—and found it long after dark. The stalls were filled, so Rex and Tarzan had to stay in the corral. I put blankets on them, and then the stable man drove me and the dog to a nearby motel. That was the poorest and most unaccommodating motel I found on the road. I'd paid there and slept cold.

I was back at the stable before dawn, had hot breakfast, then loaded and started the long trip to Burns. It was not a fit day for travel, and it would have been smart to stay over, but not at that motel.

Both the snow and the wind got worse. We came to a sawmill where there were acres of lumber. A man there asked, "What in thunder are you doing out here? Are you thinking of going to Burns today?"

"That's my idea."

"Forget it. This storm is turning into a ringtail norther. Earliest we've ever had one. The road will be blocked before you can get ten miles, and you won't see a house for twenty miles along the way. Best thing for you to do is to take the secondary about three miles up ahead. Follow it for a half mile and you'll come to a group of houses. They'll take care of you, but don't say that I sent you. They don't like me. They don't like anyone who cuts down trees."

190

We used up two hours of slow walking time to reach the secondary, and from there to the houses was the longest half mile we'd made on the trip. I hadn't noticed any downgrade, but the six or seven homes and several barns were in a sort of sheltered valley, and the storm didn't seem too bad there.

A woman came running out of the first house. They had phoned her from the sawmill and she had been watching for us. "Get down and into the house and take the dog with you," she directed. "I'll tend to the horses."

I was too near frozen to object, and Depeche Toi beat me through the door. He went right to the fireplace and stayed close to it for the next hour or so, getting warm and drying out.

A half hour passed. I was about to go to the barn when the woman came into the house.

"I had a time unstrapping your gear," she said. "You have quite a system."

"It was taught me by an efficiency expert back in Pennsylvania," I explained, but I didn't tell her that I'd improved on his efficiency along the way. "I'm surprised they phoned you from the sawmill. The man there said folks here didn't like him."

"He would say a thing like that. You were talking to my husband. He has quite a sense of humor. You plan on going on to Burns?"

"Yes. I figure I can make it before dark with an early start."

"Not in this storm. I think you'd better plan on staying right here for a few days. Wait until the road is plowed, at least."

It sounded like a rational idea to me, so I accepted her offer. We talked on about many things through the afternoon. Then her husband called and said he would stay at the mill that night, so she and I had an early supper, and then I went to bed. I hadn't slept much the night before in the cold motel, and I looked forward to a good, long sleep.

191

I had no trouble getting to sleep, but staying there proved a horse of another color. Sometime during the night, the woman started playing the piano and singing love songs at the top of her voice. Depeche Toi slept through it all, but I kept awakening. I didn't sleep at all the last hour or so before dawn. But I did think and I did listen, and I decided finally that we'd better get going for Burns, storm or no storm. I figured her husband knew what he was doing when he stayed the night at the saw mill. Her speaking voice was pleasant enough, but two or three more nights of that singing and I would have been too worn for any more travel.

We made a fine, early start for Burns. The main road had not been plowed. We didn't see a car from morning to night. We were the only things moving.

It was a dreadful day. The wind was a cutting, changing one, and half the time the snow was blinding. I had the saddles on over the blankets, Depeche Toi wore his special blanket from Spencer, Massachusetts, and I wore my parka over double wool shirts. I had never been so cold. From the very start my thumbs were almost numb. By late afternoon, I feared my mind was going numb too.

The horses plodded ahead with necks bowed. They were snow crusted in no time at all, and anyone would think they were made of snow. In places the snow had drifted and covered the fences. More than once we strayed off the road and into a field. I tried to remember to switch horses every half hour. Progress was slow, of course, and several times I tried walking ahead, but it didn't work because my legs numbed very fast.

At dusk, I spotted some house lights. I couldn't find the road into the house, so we bulled our way across country for a hundred yards or so. It was a small, one-level house, and all its lights were blazing. I knocked on both front and back doors, but nobody answered. Then I went around the house, looking in every window, but I didn't see anyone. I went around to the doors again and found both locked.

192

There was no barn there, and even if there had been one, we wouldn't have used it. That lighted, empty house gave me an uncomfortable feeling. Suddenly, I wanted to get away from there, and fast.

So it was back to the road and on toward Burns. Every time we walked up a grade I was sure that we'd see the lights of the town when we reached the top. We didn't.

We battled the weather for two more hours before we saw lights again. It was pitch black by then, and we couldn't find the path. We plowed through drifts to the house, and I scrambled up onto the porch and knocked on the door.

A window opened and a woman said, "Go on to Burns, Mister. Only four miles, and the road's not too bad from here on it. We can't take anyone in here, Mister." Then a porch light came on and she shouted, "Horses! Horses!"

The door opened and a man stepped out. A second later the woman rushed out, and a hired man appeared from nowhere. The men led the horses down to the barn, and the woman motioned to me to come into the house with Depeche Toi. The men hadn't said a word.

Inside the house the woman put her hands on her hips and stared at me before saying, "You're crazy to be out on a night like this! Where did you come from?"

"Maine."

"Oh, so you're that one? Well, I suppose you must have some brains, but you didn't use them today. You look like the next thing to frozen stiff."

"I feel that way."

"Serves you right, taking horses out in this weather. Now go into the sitting room and take off every stitch of clothing."

I went into the sitting room, but I didn't undress. I stood by the oil stove and tried to warm my bones. Depeche Toi stayed close to it, too.

When the woman came into the sitting room, she was carrying a red flannel nightgown and a blue blanket. "My name is Elsie Eisenhower," she said, "and I am not related to the President. However, he rules this country and I rule this home. Now climb out of those things before I tear them off you."

I didn't waste time doing what she asked that time. She was a big woman and looked strong enough to rule Oregon, if not the whole country. After I climbed into the gown, she wrapped the blanket around me and had me lie on a sofa near the stove. Then she hurried off and brought back some hot water bottles and tucked them around me. Off she went again to prepare some hot soup.

The back door opened and shut, and I could hear her husband ask how I was.

"She'll live," said Elsie. "The Lord is on her side. You know who she is? That crazy old woman from Maine."

"Anyone who leaves Maine can't be crazy," he said. Then he came into the sitting room and told me that his name was Henry Eisenhower. "Although of late my friends have been calling me Dwight," he added. "Say, you have two fine horses. And what sort of a Spaniel do we have here?"

"A Maine one. Mainly Spaniel and Dachshund."

He looked at me but he didn't laugh. I thought I had hatched a pretty good one. However, I never said it again.

It was seventeen below zero the next morning. Phone lines were down, all roads were blocked, and the snow was still falling. We were four miles from Burns and had no hope of getting there for days.

The Eisenhowers were half my age. But they knew Oregon winters and I didn't, so I listened to them and took their advice. The thing to do, they told me, was to forget about getting to California until spring. The winter around me was only the beginning, and it would get far worse in the months to come.

So far as they were concerned, I could sit right there with them until spring. I couldn't see it that way.

"But why not?" Elsie would say. "You're helping me with

the housework and cooking, and you're tending our horses as well as your own. We already think of you as a member of the family. Why, when spring comes, you may decide not to leave."

I was really afraid of becoming a member of that family. It would mean that they would think they owned me body and soul. I wanted to be free for the rest of my life. No strings attached. But all of it was hard to explain, so I didn't try. I had left Maine in order to be free, and I hadn't sought bonds along the way—not even when Harvey Kelsey had offered security for the rest of my days.

In the end, the Lord found the solution. The Eisenhowers had an elderly friend in Burns who took in roomers to help pay her taxes. She was lame with arthritis and found it difficult to go down the stairs and tend the furnace. When she heard about me, she offered me room and board to tend the furnace. The Eisenhowers promised to take care of the horses and Depeche Toi for me, so I accepted.

So I was working and living in the rooming house when my second Thanksgiving on the road rolled around, although I wasn't really on the road. I was sitting pretty until spring. Still, I wasn't really content. I wanted to push on to California. We were so close.

Elsie phoned me the day after Thanksgiving. She'd heard of a young couple who were driving their open truck to Alturas, California to visit relatives. They were willing to take me and the boys along. It amounted to a hundred and sixty-five miles over dangerous mountain roads. It was risky, but they thought they could make it.

I had thought of trucking before, but the rates were far more than I could afford.

"All sorts of things can happen," Elsie said. "Henry doesn't think you should risk it. Do you want to talk to Henry?"

"No," I said, "I don't have to think twice about this. I'm going."

Henry may not have known what I knew: Free trucking trips are always foreordained.

11 ☛ CALIFORNIA

In our second winter on the road, we reached California on wheels.

Rex and Tarzan wore saddles over their blankets. That was Oregon law. It was supposed to prevent the picking up of strays by thieves with trucks, but the smart thieves probably carried spare saddles.

The young couple dropped us off at the county jail in Alturas. They wanted to leave us at a hotel, but I was down to three dollars. I had purchased a few winter clothes back in Burns.

When I walked into the jail, a deputy asked me, "What are you doing here? According to the papers, you're hibernating in Oregon."

"The Eisenhowers arranged to have us trucked down."

"Really? I'll phone the sheriff. Which hotel do you want?"

"This one, if you have room," I said.

He grabbed a phone and dialed the sheriff's home number and said, "That woman from Maine just arrived from Oregon. The President of the United States arranged it! Yes! She doesn't want a hotel. She wants to stay here."

196

The sheriff said he would be right over, and the deputy arranged to stable the horses while we waited. Standing in the heated building after the long, cold ride in the truck made me drowsy, and my main concern was getting to bed. I wasn't hungry, but when the sheriff arrived, he brought a hot supper for me: Fried bacon, fried potatoes, scrambled eggs and toast. He also brought some cold meat for Depeche Toi.

The room they gave us was small and plain, but it was nice and warm and there were sheets on the bed. I slept late the next morning, and then another deputy served me breakfast.

"The Chamber of Commerce is having a fit downtown," he told me. "They're blaming the sheriff for not putting you in a hotel last night, so we're moving you into the best one in town as soon as you're ready. The dog will be a special guest, too. How is Mrs. Eisenhower?"

"It's been a hard winter for her, but she's holding up."

I had quite a time with that deputy. He kept asking questions about my friends the Eisenhowers, and I managed to give truthful answers about Henry and Elsie without revealing that they weren't the White House ones.

By noon that day, Depeche Toi and I were settled in at the hotel. I had lunch with several of the Commerce men, then accepted an invitation to see a movie at a nearby film house. The manager there said that he had read in the papers that I had never seen a talking picture. That fact was true, but I couldn't recall having told it to any reporter.

The show was hardly ten minutes old when the manager tapped me on the shoulder and said that I was wanted back at the hotel. Somebody in San Francisco wanted to talk to me on the phone. I hated to miss the rest of the talkie, but the manager said to come back anytime and see the rest. He showed it twice each afternoon.

The call at the hotel was from the Associated Press in San Francisco. The reporter wanted to know when I was leaving Alturas and what the itinerary would be.

"We leave here in the morning, if the weather is fair," I

told him. Alturas was a nice town, but it had disappointed me. For over a year we'd been headed for warm and sunny California, but up there in the Golden State's northeast corner it was just as cold as Oregon and the snow was almost as deep. "We're going to Redding as fast as we can. I'm not a mountain girl."

Then we discussed the towns along the two-hundred-mile route to Redding, and he said his company would be taking pictures of me along the way. "And what's this about the Eisenhowers hiring a truck for you? The White House refuses to comment."

"What was that? Must be something wrong. I can hardly hear you," I said. "Thanks for calling, and goodbye." I hung up the phone and went back to see the end of the movie. I never did go a third time to see the middle part. It was an interesting movie, but not as good as some of the old-time silent ones I'd seen. You couldn't have dragged Uncle Waldo to a talkie. "Why pay good money to hear women talk?" he used to say.

The long road to Redding was all uphill and down. It took us through towns named Canby and Adin on the last days in November, and then southwest through McArthur, Barney, Round Mountain and other places. All along the way, we were treated as if we were something special. It was a seldom day when we didn't have to pose for press pictures, or go on the radio or television. And every night, things were set up for us ahead of time by committees, or plain private citizens. Those Californians made us feel right at home. In a sense, they melted the winter away. It was like it had been, near the beginning in New Hampshire, only more so.

During the first few days out of Alturas both horses were carrying a touch too much weight over their bones, thanks to the hay diet back in the Eisenhower barn. So their bellies were swelled above normal, which made it rough trying to fasten the packs securely. Tarzan was well-rested and felt frisky. He wanted to jog and not walk, and the jogging kept

198

flipping the packs sideways. I rode him to keep the jogging at a minimum until he'd done some reducing.

Almost always, Depeche Toi was within sight, but far up ahead. He was the first to meet people, and it seemed like he was announcing that the rest of us were on the way. We saw more big dogs along that road than in any other state, but not a one created a fuss with Tarzan.

December 13th, my sixty-fourth birthday, passed without my knowing it. I was mixed up on my days and thought it was the 11th. My true birthday was spent in bed, just as I'd spent the previous three days. I was the ailing guest of a woman who owned an apple farm. I was down with another bad cold. She just wouldn't allow me out of that bedroom until the day after the cold broke, and all my meals were served with me propped up in bed. Almost every meal included apples which were cooked one way or another. I must have downed a bushel.

So I was sixty-four and full of apples when we went back on the road. It was the nineteenth day since we'd left Alturas and we'd covered only half the distance to Redding. It seemed like we'd never get out of the mountains.

"Redding by Christmas," I told my boys. "That means early starts and at least twenty miles a day. We can do it."

We had ten days to get there. Ten times twenty was two hundred miles, and Redding was only a hundred away; but I was playing it safe, leaving room for unexpected delays. Something always seemed to happen to delay us when we planned to get somewhere by a certain date.

Getting to Redding was important because we had a special invitation to spend Christmas there with a family. The man and his wife had driven the hundred miles to the apple ranch, where I'd been bedded, just to meet me and invite me. The apple woman hadn't let them come into my room. They had stood outside my open door and talked to me that way.

The only way to guarantee early morning starts was not to stay at private homes. Well, it seemed like even the little towns out there had rodeo grounds, and all those grounds had stables. Now we rested in rodeo stables for three nights in a row, and we would have stayed there again if a big snow storm hadn't closed in on us.

The snow turned into sleet and then back into snow again. It went on that way for hours. The slippery underfooting made the going slow and I kept a sharp lookout for a sign pointing to rodeo grounds. Then a state trooper came along and asked where we were going.

"Redding in the long run, but any place that's dry in the short run," I told him.

"There's a little farm around the next curve. I don't know who the people are, but go in there. They'll take care of you, and there's a nice barn for the horses."

"How do I know they'll have us?"

"I'm going to drop in on them right now. When they see me, they'll think they're in trouble. They'll be so relieved that I'm not there to arrest them that they'll welcome you. Be sure of it. It always works."

Well, they turned out to be the sort of people who would have welcomed any stranger. And when morning came and the storm lessened, they insisted that we stay on there until the road was safe.

"The roads are like ice and they'll be that way for days," the man predicted. "You're welcome here, but if you must get to Redding by Christmas, I'll take you there in my truck."

So that's where I was the day before Christmas: Thirty miles from Redding (thirty miles of ice). The man spent all morning fixing sideboards on his open truck and putting chains on his tires, and in the afternoon he drove us to the Redding rodeo grounds. The horses stayed in the stables there, and Depeche Toi and I checked into the Golden Eagle Hotel. I had my duffle bag with a change of clothes slung over my shoulder, and as we walked across the lobby, a man said, "One moment, please! Smile, please!"

I never did figure out how the press knew I'd go to the Golden Eagle, but the cameraman was only one of about six, and there were also reporters on hand. And while they were snapping my picture, somebody removed my old Army fatigue hat and plunked an Anzac hat down on my head.

After the press session, nobody claimed the hat. So I took over ownership and continued to wear it, instead of the fatigue, from that time on. It did things for me. I looked more like a rodeo cowgirl from Australia.

On Christmas Day, the dog and I spent most of the hours at the private home where we were the honored guests at a Christmas supper. It was more of a feast than anything else. It was a family supper, really, and it reminded me of the times when I was a little girl and the whole tribe came together for Christmas at Grandpa Libby's farm. His house was a hotel of twenty-eight rooms before he bought it, and he planned to turn it into a hotel again when he retired. But an unexplained fire burned it to the ground. Later, my folks built a small house near the cellar hole. They intended to build over the cellar at some future date, but that never happened. The small house was the one I had left behind at the start of my trip.

Back at the hotel that night, we found Mr. Fox waiting for us. He was the man who had telephoned me back in Boise about appearing on the Linkletter show. "This is a letter to you from Mr. Linkletter," he said, as he handed me an envelope. "It confirms the invitation to be on his show. When do you think you'll reach Los Angeles?"

There was no rational way to estimate that, but I took a chance and said, "Early February, if all goes well."

"Fine. We'll keep track of your progress. Please telephone Mr. Linkletter collect when you get to San Fernando, and you can discuss the date for your appearance on his show."

Mr. Fox also told me that I should be in Los Angeles several days before the show, and that Mr. Linkletter would make all arrangements for the four of us.

I studied the state map that night and decided that I'd

have to put wings on the horses to get to Los Angeles by early February. It was a far distance down the road. "We can't get an early start tomorrow, because we have to pick up our mail," I told Depeche Toi. "But after tomorrow, we'd best get cracking at every dawn."

Just as I returned to the hotel with my bundle of mail the next morning, the heavens opened up and the rain came down in buckets. By night, the weatherman was predicting three straight days of rain and the possibility of floods. Two days later, he was predicting three more days and bigger floods. I spent most of the week talking to people and selling postcards. I'd also had a new supply of cards printed. The income came in handy when I settled the bills.

On the first day of the New Year, as we walked into the first of the five hundred and fifty miles to Los Angeles, our wealth consisted of thirty-seven cents. But we were all healthy.

I'd been told all along that we'd leave winter behind us at Redding. If that's the way it was, I was far too wet to care. We walked through a cold, light drizzle for three days, and then a day of rain that was like being trapped in a waterfall. There were pools and puddles all over the main road, and some sideroads looked like rivers. The drains just couldn't handle the water. I got a good idea of what the weatherman meant by flooding. The farm fields were ponds. It was serious rain. It was trying to wash away California. If we'd had a boat, we would have made much better time.

When cars came too close, their wheels churned up water and shot it against us. Rex didn't like that one little bit. He'd skitter off to the side of the muddy shoulders, and a couple of times he almost went down. Then, when I was on Tarzan, holding the dog, a speeding truck went by us and a whole wave of water hit us. I had Rex hitched short. He panicked and reared across Tarzan's neck. Both horses went down in a muddy ditch. Depeche Toi flew over the ditch, and I ended up sitting back to back with Tarzan in a foot of muddy water. Rex was on his side, so only half his gear got a soaking. It happened on the second morning of the heavy rain, and it proved again the Lord was still on our side: None of us were hurt.

"Boys," I announced, "I apologize. I'm only sixty-four and too young to know better than to be out in weather like this. But I'm old enough not to need a second lesson. We're going to throw ourselves on the mercy of the law again and stop at the next jail."

We passed two motels in the next mile, but their daily rates were more than thirty-seven cents, and I wasn't about to ask for charity. The road went downgrade into a little town, and in the center of it we found ourselves stalled in a traffic jam. I was up on Rex and holding the dog. You couldn't see the road. Water was up to the wheel hubs on cars, and none of the cars were moving.

A woman sloshed through the water to where we were and asked if we had a place to spend the night. When I told her no, she invited us to stay at her home in the hills. "And you'd better plan to stay over several days," she said. "This rain may last for three or four. When you get a chance, turn into that sidestreet over there and follow it to the public garage. You can wait in there where it's dry until my husband comes with the truck for you. I'll phone him now."

Her place was a little ranch about ten miles back in the hills. She was Spanish and her husband was a Hindu who didn't speak much English, although he drove the truck very well. They were artists, not ranchers. In California, people called any piece of land a ranch.

Depeche Toi and I had a guest house to ourselves. The horses stayed in an open shed with the truck. We rested dry and in comfort there during four more days of heavy rain and then two extra days. The Hindu husband wouldn't let us take off until he heard over the radio that all roads to the south were safe for travel. "He doesn't approve of what you're doing," his wife confided one day, "and he thinks you should wear a veil."

I saw them at meals, for the most part. Otherwise they were busy with their art, each in a separate room. It looked to me like they didn't see much of each other, either. So I had plenty of spare time, and used up a good deal of it checking out things in my diaries (I was working on number eight by then) and trying to organize names and addresses of people I'd met. Two of the diaries were water logged, and some of my writing was hard to read.

When he decided the roads were clear, the Hindu man trucked us back to the highway and we trudged down the line through Yuba, Marysville and Lincoln, and finally into Sacramento. There we had trouble finding a place to stay, but a reporter came to the rescue and placed us, for the night, in the home of some friends. It was the first time I'd had any trouble with Depeche Toi. The people had a pet mynah bird which they had shipped in from Asia. He was black and about the size of a young Maine crow, and at night he slept with his head in a paper bag in order to keep the light from his eyes. Every time he pulled his head out of the bag, he would say something, and the dog would jump up and bark. "Martini at midnight, please," the bird would say, or "Two olives, please."

We put Depeche Toi in another room and closed the door, but he still barked every time the bird talked. I tried to teach the bird to say, "Hello, lady saddle tramp," and the closest he came, after an hour, was "Lady olive, please." I just couldn't believe the price they said they had paid for the bird. Five times as much as I had paid for Tarzan! The horse didn't talk, of course, but I felt I'd received far more on the dollar.

Now we were only three hundred and ninety-five miles from Los Angeles. There were four of us, and no one suspected that only three of us would get there.

The trouble began south of Fresno and a few miles short of Goshen. Despite traffic, we were making fair time along a wide shoulder. Then we came to a spot where a load of

204

wooden crates had toppled from a truck. Other trucks and cars had passed over the crates and smashed them, and by the time we got there the road was littered with pieces of wood.

I was up on Rex. I stopped him, gave him time to study the lumber on the road, then sent him on. I let him take his time so that he would walk between the scattered wood.

Then I heard shouts and a horn. A car full of young lunatics was coming toward us. The driver swerved, making a half moon, and scared the daylights out of Rex. He reared and jumped around and darn near went over the shoulder. Then he stood quiet, although I could feel his whole body shake.

I gave him time to calm before asking him to move. When I did, he limped. A piece of wood was stuck on his left hind foot.

It was a job getting that piece of wood loose. There was a nail stuck through it, and the end of the nail went right under Rex's shoe.

When I finally pried the wood and the nail clear, I mounted Tarzan and rode him into Goshen. Rex walked lame all the way, but that was to be expected.

We put up at a stable, and several of the horsemen inspected Rex's foot. I was afraid that part of the nail might still be in his foot, but the experts judged otherwise. "He'll be all right in a couple of days," they assured me.

Rex seemed fine the next morning. He didn't limp at all, and he certainly didn't favor that left hind foot—not even when I rode him for an hour. Still, the feeling stayed with me that it would be best to be absolutely sure the foot was clean. When I saw a big horse van pass us and pull into a gas station up ahead, I regarded it as a sign that my hunch to double-check was correct.

The van was from a horse farm near Visalia, and the driver said that his boss swore by a vet in that town. Visalia was some way from our road, but it was the closest fair-sized town, so we turned off and headed for it. When we checked into a stable there in the late afternoon, I asked the owner if he would call that certain vet.

"He's out of town and not due back until morning," the owner said. "I'm waiting for him myself. Why do you need a vet?"

When I told him about how Rex had stepped on a nail and that I suspected part of the nail might still be in that foot, the man told me that I had come to the right stable. According to him, he was the second-best horse doctor in the state. Then, by scratching with a pen knife, he found a piece of nail between the left hind hoof and the shoe. It was a tiny, rusted piece.

"He'll be all right now," the man assured me, "but I'd advise resting him a few days. Just lead him around a bit. Not that I need the business. I wasn't intending to charge you anyway. Happy to have you here."

So we remained at the stable. Rex didn't limp the following morning, but I still wanted the vet to look at him and give him a tetanus shot. Then at noon, when I asked when the vet was coming, I learned there would be a slight delay. The vet was expected home that night.

"Now stop worrying," the stableman said. "We'll get him over here tonight. There's nothing wrong with your horse, believe me. But just to ease your mind, I'll put a little turpentine on that foot."

"Isn't there another vet in town?"

"This one is the best. The others don't know half as much as I do."

So we waited until night, and then, because I kept insisting, the stable owner phoned the vet. "He'll be over first thing in the morning," the owner told me. "Said to put some carbolic acid on it, so we'll do that right now. Not as good as turpentine, in my opinion, but we'll do it anyway."

Next morning, the vet did come. He examined the foot, put some more carbolic acid on it, and said there was no danger of infection. And he said there was no need for a tetanus shot.

"Just what I told her," said the stable owner. "It was the turpentine that did the trick."

"Is it safe to have him travel?" I asked the vet.

"Absolutely. There's nothing wrong with this horse."

We set off from Visalia that same day. Rex appeared to be all right. The left hind foot seemed as sound as his other three.

My mind was relieved. The vet knew more than I did, and he said that Rex was fine and in no danger of tetanus infection. We both knew that tetanus can show up anytime from a few days to three weeks.

What we didn't know was that the infection was already in Rex's blood stream. Rex didn't know it, either.

Even if he had known it, Rex had no way of telling me.

Two afternoons later, I had a time holding Rex back. He wanted to hurry and he was nervous in traffic. And he was fidgety and danced around when I unpacked him at the fair grounds stables in Tulare. A man stepped up and held his bridle. When I thanked him for helping, he asked, "How long has he been doing this?"

"Doing what?"

"Rolling his eyes."

"Noticed it first this morning," I told him. "He was in an open-box stall facing out, and we figured something scared him during the night. The men at the stable said that kids cutting across the yard often tried to scare the horses."

"This horse needs a vet," said the man.

I went cold all over. Why hadn't I insisted on that tetanus shot the very first night? Now I stood there, mouth open, staring at the man.

"He needs a vet and you're talking to one. Let's get him inside."

After too long a wait, Rex got his tetanus shot there in Tulare. I feared it was far too late, for the infection had struck his nerves. But the vet held out hope. Rex's jaws hadn't locked, and he could manage to eat some.

The vet saw Rex at least once a day for the next sixteen days. I was the day and night nurse, feeding medication with a syringe. We did all that we could for my Tennessee boy, but he faded anyway.

I was with him in his last hour. I sat on the stall floor, near his head, stroking him. Tarzan was two stalls away, and when he started calling in a low, plaintive tone, I knew that he had sensed the end was near for his friend Rex. Somehow, horses can tell.

Dogs can, too. Depeche Toi was whining outside Rex's stall.

As I listened to the other two, Rex's body trembled, and then he was gone. I buried my face in his mane and cried.

Tarzan was still calling when I left Rex's stall. Depeche Toi waited until I came out, and then he went to Tarzan's door and whined. He wanted to make sure that his old friend was all right. I opened the door and Depeche Toi trotted in to see Tarzan.

Then I went into the stall between my two horses and tried to sleep. I was worn, but I couldn't sleep with Tarzan calling from the next stall. When he stopped finally, I still couldn't sleep.

Poor Rex. That night, I blamed myself.

I always will.

It was just the three of us again, the same as when we had started from the other coast. It was the same, but not quite the same: The heart was gone out of our trip.

We stayed on at the fair grounds in Tulare. I didn't know why, really, unless it was that I couldn't accept the fact that Rex was gone. I was almost willing to believe that the sheriff in Redding would call at any minute and say that he'd just found Rex, who had been walking back to Tennessee.

We were flat broke, and I needed bread money. I rode Tarzan into town, and sold a few cards. I hated to do it because the cards showed me up on Rex. It didn't seem right, somehow.

Then a woman gave me ten dollars. "Buy some steaks for your cute little dog. He's adorable," she said. I stopped selling cards. Depeche Toi didn't get any steaks, but he didn't mind.

Then Mr. Bell, a horse trainer at the fair grounds, invited me to his home for supper. It took a while and several invitations before I got up the courage to go. I figured I'd be sad company.

The Bell home was a big trailer, and Mrs. Bell was a fine cook. She was a great one for cooking with herbs, and no two suppers were ever alike. The Bells kept inviting me and I kept going, and their friendship finally brought me around to feeling like a human being again.

Still, it was long into February before I started thinking of continung our journey. I was real short on supplies, shorter on money, and had too much gear for one horse.

"We'll find you another horse," Mr. Bell promised.

"It will have to carry the cheapest price tag of any horse in history," I reminded him.

Well, his idea of finding me a horse was to go to the papers and explain my predicament. The press ran a number of stories. As a result, several horses were offered to me. I tried them all, but none were traffic wise. The closest I came to an experienced pack horse wasn't a horse at all: A man offered to loan me his camel. "A big truck wouldn't scare Sheba," he told me, "although Sheba might scare a truck driver."

I'd just about given up hope of finding the right horse. Then a man phoned and said he wanted me to try one of his. "My name is Elliot," he said. "This horse is a beauty. He's been in big parades and is perfectly safe anywhere. I'll pick you up in an hour." He was off the phone before I could ask the price.

An hour or so later, just as I had finished exercising Tarzan, a stableman came running up to me and said, "Senator Elliot is here to see you."

"Are you sure?" I asked. "I'm not a registered voter in California."

"You're supposed to see a horse of his."

That's how I met Senator Elliot of California. He drove me to his ranch and had me try a white horse named King. Under the coat, the horse's hide was covered with tiny black spots from his Appaloosa dam. King really was a beauty.

I rode him out on the highway, and he acted as if the cars and trucks weren't there. I couldn't find a thing wrong with that horse. He stood well when I mounted, had a nice, brisk walk, and was well mannered all around.

"What do you think of him?" asked Senator Elliot. "Will he do?"

"There's nothing wrong with King, but there might be with the price. How much?"

I came close to falling off King when I heard the price.

"And I wouldn't sell him at that low figure, but I really should cut down. I'm spending most of my time in Washington. So do you want him?"

"You're breaking my heart," I said.

"Why don't you bring Tarzan up here for a few days and let the two of them get acquainted? Now, let's go to the house. Mrs. Elliot is anxious to meet you. Oh, by the way, Art Linkletter phoned me. He's just bought King for you."

We reached Los Angeles at the end of the second week in March. Tarzan and King were made to feel at home at the Lone Ranger Stables, the fanciest excuse for stables that I'd ever seen. My boys had inside box stalls, where the best horses were kept. A horse named Silver was in the stall next to Tarzan. They got along fine.

Depeche Toi and I were put up at a big, beautiful motel in North Hollywood where there were more flower gardens than rooms. We had three rooms with a private bath, a little kitchen, and a television set. I never used the kitchen, since the motel had a fine restaurant and I was invited to eat there, but I did enjoy watching television.

I hadn't told a soul about Mesannie Hart, but now I started leading her kind of life. All the luxury and the trimmings were a far cry from the life I'd known in Maine. "Really living" was an expression I'd heard many times in my sixty-four years, and now I knew what it meant. I was really living. So was Tarzan, and Depeche Toi, and King.

We were well rested and ready for the big day of March 26th and our appearance on radio and television with Art Linkletter. The whole day was mapped out for us. I was at the stable early to help load the horses in the van for the ride to the broadcasting studio. That was the time Tarzan decided to declare his independence. For some strange reason, he didn't want to go anywhere or do anything. It was almost as if he didn't want to leave Silver.

So that's why Tarzan wasn't on the Linkletter show. I was supposed to ride King onto the set, but I ended up leading him. They were afraid King might slip.

We had a great time on that show with Mr. Linkletter. From his introduction, you would have thought that our trip was more important than the one Columbus made. He asked questions and I answered them to the best of my ability, although some of the answers may not have made much sense. I was looking into those cameras full face (in case movie producers were watching!) and that was the reason Mr. Linkletter had to repeat a couple of questions.

After the show, he gave me "a little check to buy a new saddle for King." I didn't look at the check until I was back in the motel. Either the man knew little about the cost of saddles in California, or he thought a horse should wear a different saddle every day of the week. I knew there was that much money in the world, but I'd never held it in my hand.

211

It was enough to buy a new saddle and also make the living easy for the four of us for quite some time.

"Where to now?" asked the reporter from the Associated Press.

"Long Beach," I said. "Depeche Toi and I have reached our goals, but Tarzan here has a little unfinished business. He still has to wet his feet in the Pacific."

The distance Tarzan had walked from Minot to Los Angeles was close to seven thousand miles, and I had sat on top of him for two thousand of them.

According to my diaries, we had been through eighteen states on our seventeen-month journey. As far as Tarzan was concerned, some of the miles he had walked had been unnecessary: Eleven hundred miles spent on side trips to visit certain places or people. The total of seven thousand miles was a short figure in his case, of course, for I had no way of knowing the number of miles he had covered during his runaway sprees with Rex.

I had stopped keeping a record of our mileage when we reached Los Angeles, but we started adding many more to it the day we struck off for Long Beach. There we found a pretty beach, and Tarzan washed his feet in the Pacific Ocean—with me on top of him, King at his side, and Depeche Toi barking at the waves. We stood there in the water for ten minutes or so, then walked along the beach a ways before making a turn for the coast road.

As we passed the beach police station, an officer stepped out and said, "I saw you on the Linkletter show. You were very entertaining."

"Thank you."

"You didn't squint in all those lights. How is your vision?"

"Perfect, so far as I know," I told him. "Never worn glasses in my life."

"Then how come you missed all the signs on the road side

212

of the beach? Horses aren't allowed on this beach. It's against the law. This beach is only for bathers."

"Show me a sign," I said, and he did. We weren't twenty feet from one. The fine was fifty dollars a horse.

"The law is strictly enforced," the officer told me. "But I can't see two feet without my glasses, and I don't know where I've misplaced them. Now get out of here and enjoy California before I find them."

I smiled my thanks and we got out of there, but the joke was on him; he didn't know we had official permission to do this. We saved a hundred dollars that day, although I wouldn't have paid it. I would have served time in jail instead. It would have been a crime to pay anything more for washing Tarzan's feet in the Pacific. He had already paid seven thousand miles to do so.

After Long Beach, we lazied around the nearby territory, staying a day here and two days there, and always with people who had invited us to visit them, after seeing us on that Linkletter show. Then we headed back for Los Angeles. I was anxious to look over the new mail waiting for us there.

As we trudged along through South Pasadena, a canary yellow sports car passed us and pulled to the curb up ahead. The driver was a woman. She wore dark glasses, had flaming red hair, and her clothes appeared real expensive. She looked for all the world like a movie star to me, but she wasn't.

She was a young, lady lawyer, and she had a proposition for me. I could live in her house as long as I liked, and she would pay all my day-to-day living expenses, such as food for the four of us. She explained she was often out of town on business trips, and hated to leave the house unoccupied for fear of robbery. She owned certain paintings and other valuable things. The way she put it, we would be doing her a favor just by living at her place.

So we paid her the favor—Depeche Toi and I moved into her house, and the horses were stabled within easy walking distance at her expense. Now I had a more or less permanent address, and the movie people would know where to look if they wanted me. That's what I told myself after reading my new mail, anyway. It didn't contain any movie offers.

A week or so later, I decided to ride Tarzan through Pasadena for a look at the famous Rose Bowl. As we waited for a street light to change to green, a young man stepped off the curb and asked if we could talk for a minute. He explained that he had been looking for me, and that he was an agent for actors.

"Hollywood is shooting a great many westerns these days, and I can land you some big character roles," he said. "Ever done any acting?"

"All my life, pretty much," I said. I meant that I had acted the fool.

"You'll need a new name, probably. Mesannie Wilkins doesn't sound right for an actress."

"My acting name is Mesannie Hart. Ever hear of William S. Hart?"

"A relative? Really? Why this is perfect! What's your phone number?"

I gave it to him. Then he told me to stay by the telephone from ten o'clock to two every weekday until I heard from him.

I promised to do just that, and I did. But I never heard from him, and around the end of April, when I was in a supermarket, I came face to face with him. He apologized for not calling me, then told me that he had become an actor.

"I've been so busy with my own career, that I forgot about yours," he eplained. "But I have an agent now, and he's a good one. I'll tell him about you. You have a great future in westerns. Your publicity should get you into every studio. What's your phone number again?"

I waited into May, but the new agent didn't phone. Outside of riding the horses every day and selling a few cards, there wasn't much for me to do. So I started studying my eight diaries of the trip and the envelopes and cards I'd collected, and getting names and addresses in order. Sooner or later, I meant to write all the people who'd been nice to us along the way, and to the hundreds of others we'd never met but who had invited us to stay at their homes. I figured I'd had a year's supply of invitations from Texas alone.

"How would you like to visit Texas?" I asked Depeche Toi one day.

He gave me one of those "Not again!" looks and trotted from the room.

Later that day, I saddled Tarzan and rode him to the nearest gas station for a new supply of road maps.

It had taken me more than six decades to realize the fact, but now I knew that I had been born restless.

It all happened more than twelve years ago, and I'll always be thankful that we made the journey.

We found America full of wonderful people. Those foreigners who don't like us should try meeting us on our home grounds.

By now, I should have written all those people whom I'd met, and all those others who invited me to visit them. But you lose things when you travel light and move around, and I still haven't settled down. Pages from diaries are missing, and so are three of the diaries. So what I've written here is from the other diaries, and from notes on scraps of paper and envelopes, and from the way I've remembered things.

All of the names should be correct, except for one: Harvey Kelsey. His real name is a private matter, of course.

I haven't been back to Maine, but it's been getting along real well without me. Mrs. Miller is gone now, and so are other old friends. I don't know if the doctor who gave me "four more years" is still there.

And I haven't been back to Wyoming. So far as I know, Harvey is still waiting. Sometimes, during lonely spells, I'm tempted to go back there and join him, and maybe I will some day. I never was one to rush into things.

Other titles in the Equestrian Travel Classic series published by
The Long Riders' Guild Press. We are constantly adding to our
collection, so for an up-to-date list please visit our website:
www.thelongridersguild.com

Title	Author
Southern Cross to Pole Star – Tschiffely's Ride	Aime Tschiffley
Tale of Two Horses	Aime Tschiffley
Bridle Paths	Aime Tschiffely
This Way Southward	Aime Tschiffely
Bohemia Junction	Aime Tschiffely
Through Persia on a Sidesaddle	Ella C. Sykes
Through Russia on a Mustang	Thomas Stevens
Across Patagonia	Lady Florence Dixie
A Ride to Khiva	Frederick Burnaby
Ocean to Ocean on Horseback	Williard Glazier
Rural Rides – Volume One	William Cobbett
Rural Rides – Volume Two	William Cobbett
Adventures in Mexico	George F. Ruxton
Travels with A Donkey in the Cevennes	Robert Louis Stevenson
Winter Sketches from the Saddle	John Codman
Following the Frontier	Roger Pocock
On Horseback in Virginia	Charles Dudley Warner
California Coast Trails	J. Smeeton Chase
My Kingdom for a Horse	Margaret Leigh
The Journeys of Celia Fiennes	Celia Fiennes
On Horseback through Asia Minor	Fred Burnaby
The Abode of Snow	Andrew Wilson
A Lady's Life in the Rocky Mountains	Isabella Bird
Travels in Afghanistan	Ernest F. Fox
Through Mexico on Horseback	Joseph Carl Goodwin
Caucasian Journey	Negley Farson
Turkestan Solo	Ella K. Maillart
Through the Highlands of Shropshire	Magdalene M. Weale
Wartime Ride	J. W. Day
Across the Roof of the World	Wilfred Skrede
Woman on a Horse	Ana Beker
Saddles East	John W. Beard
Last of the Saddle Tramps	Messanie Wilkins
Ride a White Horse	William Holt
Manual of Pack Transportation	H. W. Daly
Horses, Saddles and Bridles	W. H. Carter
Notes on Elementary Equitation	Carleton S. Cooke
Cavalry Drill Regulations	United States Army
Horse Packing	Charles Johnson Post
14th Century Arabic Riding Manual	Muhammad al-Aqsarai
The Art of Travel	Francis Galton
Shanghai à Moscou	Madame de Bourboulon
Saddlebags for Suitcases	Mary Bosanquet
The Road to the Grey Pamir	Ana Louise Strong
Boot and Saddle in Africa	Thomas Lambie
To the Foot of the Rainbow	Clyde Kluckhohn
Through Five Republics on Horseback	George Ray
Journey from the Arctic	Donald Brown
Saddle and Canoe	Theodore Winthrop
The Prairie Traveler	Randolph Marcy
Reiter, Pferd und Fahrer – Volume One	Dr. C. Geuer
Reiter, Pferd und Fahrer – Volume Two	Dr. C. Geuer

The Long Riders' Guild
The world's leading source of information regarding equestrian exploration!
www.thelongridersguild.com